√SOU

BU

Date Due

JAN 2 0 1998			
MAR 1 2 1998			
JUN 2 6 '98			
JUL 1 3 '98			
OCT 27 '98			
NOV 2 7 '98			
AUG 1 0 '00			
NOV 23 01			
OCT 3 0 2003			

3/06 - to Ash

1 / 98

01~

Jackson
County
Library
Services

HEADQUARTERS
413 W.Main
Medford, Oregon 97501

Food Fights

Food Fights

Tales from the Restaurant Trade

STORIES BY

FRED BONNIE

Black Belt Press

Montgomery

Black Belt Press
P.O. Box 551
Montgomery, AL 36101

Some of these stories have appeared in the following magazines and literary
journals: *Birmingham, Portland, Bozart, Confrontation, Oktoberfest,* and *The
Fiddlehead.* Thanks to Tony's Pizza and Pit Restaurant, Montgomery,
Alabama, for use of their menu art on the divider pages.

Library of Congress Cataloging-in-Publication Data
Bonnie, Fred.
   Food fights : stories / by Fred Bonnie.
      p. cm.
      ISBN 1-881320-73-1
   1.Restaurants--Fiction. 2. Food habits--Fiction. I. Title.
PS3552.0637F66 1997
813'.54--dc21   97-924
                                                                                CIP

Design by Randall Williams
Printed in the United States of America
97 98 99 00   5 4 3 2 1

*The Black Belt, defined by its dark, rich soil, stretches across central
Alabama. It was the heart of the cotton belt. It was and is a place of
great beauty, of extreme wealth and grinding poverty, of pain and joy.
Here we take our stand, listening to the past, looking to the future.*

To my brothers, Nick, Bill, and BJ, cookers all;
and to the 9.4 million people currently
employed in the U.S. food and
beverage industry.

Then the Lord said unto Moses, Behold, I will rain bread from heaven for you; and the people shall go out and gather a certain rate every day, that I may prove them, whether they will walk in my law, or no.

Exodus 16:4

And into whatsoever city ye enter, and they receive you, eat such things as are set before you.

Luke 10:8

Bill of Fare

Tony's

Appetizers

I

He poked around in the paper sack I handed him through the window, taking out the napkins and the eight plastic ketchup packets. He held the drink cup up in front of his eyes with two fingers, as if he'd discovered a disease on it. Then he turned his stare toward me as if he had a stiff neck. His hair stuck straight out from under the crown of his hat, and now he leaned far out of the window of his dented red pickup.

"You screwed up my order."

"Beg pardon?"

"I wanted French fries, not these goddam potato patty things."

"Sorry . . . "

"Get it right, Idiot." He looked away.

I was told once, maybe back when I was a kid selling magazine subscriptions, to try to make the customer laugh if he's angry.

"What if I told you I didn't really give a shit what you want, but that I was going to give it to you anyway, just to show you what a great guy I am?"

He looked at me with a powerful blankness, tilting his head back just enough for me to see the whole flat oval of his face and its angry creases that were deep enough to suck me in and lose me. I stared back, but I knew I could never match his granite blankness. I was just glad he didn't know my address.

It was my first day, and this bozo looked like a real regular. Maybe GM would reopen the plant, fire up the line, and hire me back on my old job before the morning was over.

II

He stood at the edge of the booth, leaning into it with his thighs. The bead curtain draped over his shoulders and back. "Where you learn say *shay-shay* mean thank you?"

"Eating in Chinese restaurants."

He reared upward and backward, as if he might fall over and bring the bead curtain down with him, but he caught himself and now leaned toward the booth again, a few strands of the beads draped down his front. He was young, his hair glistened blackly, his contorted teeth made him look a bit demented but in a friendly way. His lips curled back in total approval.

"You speaka ver *good* Chinese."

· "I only know three or four words."

"Oh no, I think you know much more. I think you maybe speaka Chinese fru-en-ree."

He brought the wonton soup, and after he set it down, he continued to stand by the booth. "Tell me alla Chinese word you know?"

"Hen how chuh."

The waiter laughed wildly, bowing, straightening, bowing again, making a lot of noise when he laughed. "Ha ha, hen how chuh. So delicious, isn't it?" His laugh abruptly stopped. "You ever go China?"

"No."

"You go China, you stay my family home."

"I don't think I'll be going soon."

"Serious. You stay my family."

"They don't know me."

"Is not important. You go China, you stay my family. I write address for you. You have piece a paper?"

The steam of the soup rose to my nose. I motioned to him with my finger to lean closer. He brought his face over the soup, his ear near my mouth as I whispered.

"I'm a convicted murderer and rapist. I just got out of prison this afternoon. You sure you want me under the same roof with your mother and sisters, aunts and grandmothers?"

I saw that he didn't understand. His face registered a moment of puzzlement, then brightened again. "I bling you egg lowl now. My family gonna so glad to see you."

III

The guitarist is so bad he's good. I mean, he's got a real *schtick*. He knows every corny song—"Goodnight Irene," "I Remember Mama," "Volare." He goes from table to table, booth to booth. He's bad enough when he's strumming, but then he tries to pick out a solo. Just plain friggin' awful. His voice is emotional and quivery, and his big, bulging eyes kind of roll back when he's *really* into it. His breath—you could light it with the candle on the table. He keeps leaning into our faces and almost falling in my lap.

Maybe it's a mistake, but I clap for him, even when he moves off to play to another table. I have to; I used to be a drummer in a country band. I always clap. Usually I'm the only one in the house who knows when they finish a number.

So he keeps coming back to our booth. Sally's irked. She likes a lot of things in life better than music. It's all background to her, but this guy refuses to be background.

"I hate it when you do this," she says, eyeing Mario as he smiles toward us, hesitates, comes back.

"Whaddya wanna hear this time?"

"Sing that Beatles song," Sally pipes up. "Something about doing it in the road?"

Mario blanks, strums once. "Ain't it awful the way they ruin music these days?" He starts "That's Amore," but the owner comes over and points around the place, talking in Italian. I don't know the lingo, but I know he's cussing.

Mario don't finish the song; he just sets his guitar in a corner, picks up a tray, starts busing tables. That's his real job, it turns out. Man, talk about a personality change. He ain't smiling and chatty anymore, just kind of sad and beaten-down, lugging that tray of dirty dishes.

I'm going back to that joint one of these days and I'm gonna smack that bastard for making a musician bus tables. I don't care *how* lousy the guy plays.

IV

"Say, don't you have menus in this place?"

The waiter, dressed in a gray Mao tunic and sandals, looked as if he'd spent his entire life wanting to be Chinese. He bowed again.

"No, sir. You must cast the yarrow stalks, and that will determine which of our sixty-four menu items you will be served. Or, if you prefer, you may cast coins rather than yarrow stalks. We hope one day to be able to heat a tortoise shell and decide what you'll eat based on an interpretation of the cracks in the shell."

"Oh, how wonderful. I can't imagine what the holdup might be?"

"The health department," he continued seriously. "And finding a reliable supplier of the correct tortoise."

So I cast the coins. The waiter told me that I'd tossed a number fifty-five.

"What's that?"

"Abundance," the waiter announced with evident pride. "You get an entire roast pig." He smiled, but only for a moment. "However, you have a changing line in your hexagram. The new configuration is number sixty-one. Inner Truth."

"What's that?"

"Liver and onions. You may order either the pig or the liver. Your pleasure, of course."

"Just out of curiosity, what's a . . . lets say . . . a number eight?"

"Ah . . . Holding Together. This is tomato aspic."

"Can I try the coins again?"

"Oh, no sir. One must never doubt the accuracy of the ancient and revered oracle."

I stood up. "Look, this place is too complicated. I've got to get back to work." I decided to order my age. "Give me a number forty-eight to go."

"Very good, sir. Number forty-eight is The Well. Do you prefer your cup of water with or without ice?"

V

"Wha chew want, Hon?"

"I don't know yet." Ellis looked at the menu, trying to appear uninterested in the waitress when he was really there to study her again. In his periphery he swept in her broad hips and droplet-stained uniform. It struck Ellis as the uniform of a nurse rather than that of a waitress— white pants, lapelled white blouse and apron, white denim shoes that spread to the sides and split in small cracks just above the soles. Her dark brown hands always held her order pad and pen, but Ellis knew she would not write down his or anyone else's order. He'd watched her take a dozen orders at a time and never write one down. She carried the pad to each booth, then tossed it on the counter by the cash register as she jabbed the pen into the carpet of orange curls on her head and hollered the orders to an imaginary kitchen staff, then stepped behind the counter to coax the eggs or paint the pancake batter onto the griddle, or fly her fingers over the toasters as she dealt slices of bread into the slots.

In that moment when she hollered the orders to herself, she stood erect and military, as if she were reporting on behalf of the entire platoon, name by name, to some sergeant she had known once.

VI

Mason didn't think the food at The Golden Dragon was very good. He had come back a second time only because he thought the cashier was possibly the most beautiful girl he'd ever seen in his life. He watched her tilt her head to one side to keep her long, straight hair out of her face as she concentrated on the keys of the cash register, pushing them one at a time between glances at the customer check. It was over a week since Mason had been here—her first night on the job, she'd confided—and she was still clearly struggling. The white-shirted owner, most of his tie tucked between his shirt buttons, had to come out from the kitchen to help her ring up every other check. They spoke together in bad English, so Mason guessed she was probably not Chinese, maybe Korean; too tall, he'd decided, to be Vietnamese.

Mason thought it was sad the way she constantly glanced up at the clock, lifted a slat of the Venetian blind to look out into the parking lot, and paced the few steps between the cash register and the door, wobbling dangerously on her high heels. She seemed uncomfortable in her long, tight, red polyester dress. She looked at Mason often with her bright, erratic smile.

His muscles tensed and his heart lodged itself in his throat when she came to his table and stood a few feet away.

"So bore," she said.

There were only four other customers. It was not a pretty Chinese restaurant; the cheaply panelled walls were unadorned. There were no pretty lamps hanging from the ceiling, no plastic dragons nailed to the walls.

"Boss so awful. Say I have to pour water for customer. I lee-fuse. Tell him that is waitress work. I am cashier."

Mason said nothing, only watched.

She moved closer. "You wanna give me ride home? Maybe take me on date first?"

Mason's heart clattered inside him. He could only nod and rasp. "Sure."

She disappeared into the kitchen. Angry voices echoed out into the dining area, growing louder as the owner, his face and shirt soaked, followed her, talking rapidly in Chinese. She walked in short, quick steps to Mason's table, smiling serenely, her hand extended to take his.

"Come on. We go now."

Outside, she hooked her arm through his as they walked.

"Pour the water is waitress work," she said again. "I am too educated person. You agree?"

"I believe you're extremely well educated."

She patted his arm. "Thass right. You, too."

VII

By five in the morning, the Algerians were already up, waiting for the first traces of daylight to start work. They were all construction workers, allowed into France by the government as immigrant laborers. Their wives were not allowed to accompany them. A construction crew of fifteen or twenty men erecting a high-rise condominium or office complex would quickly complete a single ground-floor room of the building in which they would all live while they worked for a year or more to complete the remaining ten or fifteen stories.

They gathered for breakfast at a Tunisian cafe just off Avenue Jean Medecin, where they drank strong coffee and ate North African pastries that were dipped in honey then coated with ground almonds. From a tiny radio next to the cash register, the tinny wails of a quavering singer wafted just above the hushed voices of the customers. Two walls of the room were painted in a continuous scene of sea and clouds. The third wall had a few white stucco buildings, a lone grazing camel, and three pyramids. The fourth wall was the window that faced the avenue, which was deserted at that hour of the morning.

The Algerians always turned around, nearly in unison, to watch Russell whenever he entered the cafe and went to the counter to order a cup of coffee and a pastry to carry back to his hotel room. The owner, a thin-cheeked man with slicked-back hair and a curly beard, greeted Russell with a smile and a handshake while the customers stared.

"You finish school yet?" Abdul asked, as he did every morning when Russell stopped there.

"Someday."

"Where will you make vacation after school?"

It was a new question, and Russell realized he had no hope of answering well. "I hadn't thought about it."

"Go to Tunisia. You been there?"

"No."

"The best part is the women." Abdul touched the tip of his finger to his tongue then touched Russell's cheek. "Sssss," he hissed. "They are so hot they can *burn* you."

Russell noticed that the place had fallen to silence and that all eyes watched, all ears listened. "Sounds kind of interesting," he said. "But I'm married."

The silence held another moment, then Abdul began to laugh. Russell looked around the cafe. The men all smiled and nodded. Russell wondered exactly what part of his answer had so pleased them, and he guessed it must have been the part about going nowhere near the women they'd left alone back home to receive their laborers' checks.

Tony's

Entrees

Broom of Destruction

ISAIAH HAD been brought up by his momma to feel like a prophet, and now, as he watched the new cook through the chute where the waitresses stacked the dirty dishes, Isaiah had a premonition that the guy wouldn't even last the night.

Davis was his name. "As in Jefferson *Davis* Drummond," he had corrected when Mr. Pinkas, the owner, introduced the new cook as Jeff Drummond. Isaiah watched out of the corner of his eye when Jefferson Davis Drummond drifted into the kitchen, sucked along in the wake of the chubby, scurrying Mr. Pinkas. Davis had his shoulders thrown back and his middle sucked in. Yellow flattop, gold hoop earring. His pale white smile twitched at the corners of his mouth as he looked Isaiah over in a single vertical flicker of his eyes.

Isaiah didn't have to suck his stomach in to look thin, like Davis did. He figured Davis outweighed him by fifty pounds, maybe more. And Isaiah got the message in that smile all right; the black dishwasher was to jump when the white short-order cook said so.

Now, as Isaiah peered through the dish chute, he saw that Davis planned to spread his authority over the waitress, Shyreena, as well. What was Davis telling her, Isaiah wondered. That she was to address him as *sir* at all times?

"I will take vengeance on my foes," whispered Isaiah. "And fully repay my enemies."

Isaiah had long regretted that Shyreena was so good looking. She was dark and thick in the mouth and hips, with cornrow hair and big, sneering, rolling white eyes, just as Isaiah liked his women. He'd told her not to walk so slow and swaying when other men were around, and not to smile at them like she heard sex in every damned thing anybody said to her. It was just habit, she told him, kind of like looking at ice cream and not knowing you're smiling. She'd been walking and talking and smiling that way all her life, especially since she was fourteen. "And that's why you twenty and got two kids and a ex-husband that act like he Casper the ghost," Isaiah had replied.

Now this yellow-haired honkey sitting out there in a booth folding napkins with Shyreena—not one of the cook's jobs—and Shyreena, damn her pecan-colored ass, laughing and blinking with Davis and telling him he looked like a *Pisces* she used to know, and wasn't he a Pisces, too, since he looked like a fish? Laugh laugh. Not Davis, just her.

The daughters of Zion are haughty, Isaiah thought to himself. They walk with necks outstretched, ogling and mincing.

Isaiah went out into the dining area, dragging his broom behind him. A lone customer sat at the counter and two more sat in a booth. Davis took out a deck of cards and started dealing them. "Two out of three," Davis said, smiling at her, the red in his face almost jolly.

"Or until I win," Shyreena said, her make-believe hard look on.

"That steam table don't clean itself," Isaiah said.

Davis slowly looked up, smirking as always. Isaiah tried to keep his face neutral. "Have it your way," Isaiah said. "But you on your own as far as I'm concerned."

"Always was, Sport."

Isaiah knew he had Davis going, and Davis proved it, the way he smiled. Isaiah pressed on. "You better get the grill cleaned and stocked up good before that movie across the way gets out."

Davis started laying the cards out, face up, giving a little speech about each one, and Isaiah saw that Davis was doing Shyreena's Tarot. Isaiah knew about Tarot. His mother had been a palm reader during most of his childhood. He could see that Davis was a pitiful amateur.

Shyreena hunched her head into her shoulders and swung her eyes back and forth over the cards. "I got all the romance in my life that I want *or* need," she wheezed, dipping her head toward the table and nodding like an old woman. She still didn't look at Isaiah, but she didn't look at Davis either.

"I heard that," Davis said, craning to look down the front of her white, loose-necked blouse.

She sat back up quickly and her bracelets clinked like something way back in the wind as she drummed her fingers near her stack of napkin-wrapped silverware. Shyreena sneered with her upper lip and one pencilled eyebrow.

"Is that all them silly-ass cards of yours got to say? *Ro*mance?" She glanced up at Isaiah and smiled. "You talk romance to me, White Boy, and my main man here will *get* you, huh baby? He don't carry that broom of destruction for decoration."

Davis looked up from his cards, his smile no longer coy but toothy and mean. "Ooooo. I gotta take a *fright* break."

THE MOVIE WAS just getting out, and the restaurant quickly filled with noisy kids, black as well as white, who poured quarters into the juke box, then demanded that the volume be turned up to maximum. They almost always managed to clog the commodes with paper towels, then whined that the toilets wouldn't flush. Most of them wanted hamburgers, and Isaiah made it a practice to show the new cooks he happened to like how to get set up ahead of time by cooking the beef patties and keeping them warm in the oven. But Isaiah didn't plan to help Davis in any way.

During the rush, Isaiah leaned against the dishwashing machine, watching Davis get more and more frantic. It was obvious to Isaiah that Davis wasn't as experienced as he'd claimed to be earlier that afternoon when Mr. Pinkas hired him. Whenever Davis dropped a french fry or a pickle slice on the floor, Isaiah flicked it away with his broom, which he always kept within reach.

"What the shit you staring at?"

"The sweat you dripping all over that food," Isaiah said. "I'm glad I ain't the one that's gonna eat it."

Davis slid two plates of food onto the counter for Shyreena to pick up, pinged the little bell there, then leaned against the counter with his thumbs hooked over the string of his white apron as he faced Isaiah.

Isaiah smirked back.

Shyreena, who never moved as if she were in a hurry, floated back and forth between the kitchen and the dining area with the plates of food that Davis put out. He was way behind, and now she leaned against the frame of the open kitchen door waiting for her orders, one hip angled out.

"I *Zay* Uh, baby," she crooned, "I'm gonna need some mustard pretty soon. You hear me? I *Zay* Uh?"

Isaiah took his broom and brushed by Shyreena's hip. "Bitch," he whispered.

THE CELLAR WAS Isaiah's private domain. Only he and Mr. Pinkas ever went down there. Shyreena used to get her own napkins and condiments when she first came to work at The Oasis, but now she refused to go downstairs ever since Isaiah had told her that once in awhile he had to kill a rat. That, he had told her, was the main reason he always carried his broom with him.

To make sure no one else came downstairs, Isaiah kept the lightbulb unscrewed so that the switch at the top of the stairs didn't work. In the dark, he made his way to the walk-in, flailing with his hands as if he were blind. It was a game he often played in the dark. Could he make it in life if he were blind? He was sure he could. Now Isaiah clenched his jaws and thought about Shyreena and Davis.

"The people who walked in darkness have seen a great light," he mumbled.

He pulled open the heavy, metal door of the walk-in refrigerator and snapped on the light. Whisps of steam slowly rose from the cold vats like adders swaying out of their baskets. Rage always made him hungry, and now he eyed the cellophane-covered vats and a platter of roast beef as he brooded. With the French knife he kept on the shelf, Isaiah speared himself several slices of the pink meat and crammed it slice by slice into his mouth, working it with his angry jaws. Then he brushed the

cellophane back and stuffed a handful of pasta salad into his mouth as his
eyes roamed over the small horizon of platters and vats before him.

A side of beef hung at the far end of the walk-in, waiting to be
butchered by Mr. Pinkas. Isaiah tried to imagine the red slab of meat
with legs and horns and a tail and eyes that would look at him with that
detached curiosity that only cows possessed. He had never seen a cow,
except in a magazine once. It was the cow's eyes that caught his attention,
large and dull, full of great quantities of nothing.

"In the blood of calves, lambs, and goats I find no pleasure," he
murmured.

He continued to eat anyway. As he chewed, the image of Shyreena
taunting Davis clawed at him. He listened to his mind another moment,
then the fury began to pound in his neck and shoulders. In the side of
beef he no longer saw a dull-witted cow; instead, he saw the torso and
smirk of Davis.

When Isaiah could tell by the level of noise coming from above that
the rush was over, he went back upstairs. Only a single booth of teenagers
remained. He quickly bussed the tables and loaded all the dishes into the
dishwasher. He couldn't wash the vats and pots from supper, though,
because Davis still hadn't broken down the steam table.

Isaiah dragged the broom toward the door and began to sweep. He
clunked the broom louder than usual among the stems of the stools at the
counter. When he finished sweeping, he got a mop and some rags from
the kitchen and went to clean the restrooms. He made a constant noise
with the mop, bumping the walls as he swabbed. Serving notice on
Davis. In the two years that Isaiah had worked there, he had seen six
cooks and as many waitresses come and go. Only Isaiah stayed on, which
was why Mr. Pinkas had him train each new cook, whether the cooks
liked taking orders from the dishwasher or not.

Isaiah came out of the women's bathroom and glanced at the clock
above the coffee urns. It was almost 10:40. The jukebox continued to
play, although the last booth of customers had left.

So, too, it appeared, had Shyreena and Davis. They were not in the
dining room, nor did Isaiah see them in the still kitchen. His rage flew to

his brain and his hand gripped the broom as he thundered down the stairs to the cellar.

Isaiah summoned all his strength to throw open the heavy door to the walk-in refrigerator. The thick, metal slab slammed against the wall, and Isaiah imagined that it shook the entire building.

"He shall strike the ruthless with the rod of his mouth," Isaiah bellowed. "And with the breath of his lips he shall slay the wicked."

He picked up his broom and swung the head at the side of beef. The thud puffed his rage to dizziness, and he swung the broom again.

"For this I will make the heavens tremble, and the earth shall be shaken from its place," Isaiah roared. "The wrath of the Lord blazes against his people, he raises his hand to strike them; when the mountains quake, their corpses shall be like refuse in the streets!"

Isaiah swung the broom again and again. When it broke, he grabbed the French knife from the shelf and charged at the side of beef, stabbing and kicking.

"Behold the Lord of hosts lops off the boughs . . . The Lord shall shave with the razor hired from across the river the head and the hair between the legs . . ."

He stopped for a moment, dizzy, his chest heaving, his eyes hot and watery. As Isaiah crumpled to his knees on the cold floor of the walk-in, he thought he heard footsteps behind him, fleeing up the stairs. The side of beef swung on its hook, large chunks sagging like tongues from its sides.

The noise of the restaurant grew in Isaiah's ears as he swayed at the foot of the stairs, exhausted, wanting to stay in the cellar and lie down on the stack of dirty aprons and kitchen rags in the storeroom. But he forced himself up, step by step.

Shyreena was in the kitchen.

"Where you been?" Isaiah demanded. "After I cleaned them bathrooms, you was gone."

"I was showing Davis the garbage cans in the alley." She looked pale, harried. "I got customers . . ."

Isaiah's chest heaved. He could hardly speak. "So, go wait on them."

Isaiah looked into the kitchen, then at Shyreena. His mind and energy began to seep back. "Where's the cook at?"

Shyreena was already back out front.

Isaiah decided to just go ahead and do the work tonight and get Davis fired in the morning. He went into the kitchen and began slapping hamburger patties onto the hot griddle.

"I need seven more hamburgers," Shyreena said.

"Where *is* that damned cook?"

"I dunno. He just took off on out of here when he come back upstairs."

"He was downstairs?"

Shyreena kept her eyes away. "I sent him down for . . ."

"He was downstairs?" Isaiah repeated. He studied her a moment before he let his feet break into a shuffle as he deftly flipped the two rows of meat patties. "I will take vengeance on my foes, saieth the Lord of hosts!" he laughed.

Shyreena frowned as she arranged three platters on her left arm and picked up two more with her right hand. "Just cook them burgers, okay?"

Isaiah watched her lurch toward the booths and wondered why she suddenly seemed so tired and her voice sounded so flat and angry. He pointed his spatula at her back.

"Don't you be poking your neck out like no daughters of Zion," he ordered her, quietly.

A Live Maine Lobster

VINCE PACED in his wheelchair along the row of empty window-side booths as he waited for the insurance man to arrive. The afternoon sun filled the window, and Vince squinted at the cars that came and went in the street, disapproving, as always, of the many foreign cars he saw. Vince regarded most foreign vehicles as something less than real cars; they were just too damned small to be taken seriously.

There were a few exceptions. Vince was stationed in Germany in the 1950s, and he'd once driven a Mercedes. That was a real car. But the most truly real car on the road was a Cadillac. Vince had always been a Cadillac lover.

"A ten-year-old old Caddy is ten times as classy as a brand-new Chevy," Vince's Uncle Yoni used to say. Vince had owned dozens of Caddies over the years, some of which ran and some of which didn't. But at least he'd owned them. Vince maintained that just sitting in a Caddy was better than actually going somewhere in one of these Japanese things.

So when the insurance man pulled up in front of the restaurant in a shiny red Japanese car, Vince instantly disliked him. Vince disliked anyone who carried a briefcase or wore loafers with tassels or had blond hair, clipped close on top but long and shaggy at the back and sides.

Vince wheeled himself toward the locked door and turned the latch to let the insurance man in. It was a dialysis day, and the ambulance had dropped Vince at Brad's restaurant rather than bring him home. For a few hours after his treatments, Vince actually felt pretty good. He didn't like being home alone when he felt good, only when he felt bad. Then he wanted to be alone so no one would see how he was when he felt bad. It seemed to Vince that it would be easier for the insurance man to meet him at the restaurant rather than have to drive all the way out to Brad's apartment.

Now Bob whatever-his-name-was smiled incessantly as he introduced himself, giving Vince two more things to dislike: the guy smiled when there was no reason to; plus, Vince had just never cared much for people named Bob.

Vince pointed to the booth nearest the window. Bob sat down and lay his briefcase on the seat beside him.

"So, you're from California, huh?"

"No," said Vince. "I've been *living* in California. I'm *from* the state of Maine."

"Whoa, that's a change. What brings you to Alabama?"

"I'd sooner file my fingernails with a chainsaw than spend one more god-awful winter in the state of Maine."

Bob laughed, much too hard for what the remark was worth, in Vince's estimation.

"Besides, the state of California wanted to unload me from their Medicaid rolls. Since I'm not a real Californian, whatever in hell *that* is."

Bob nodded gravely. "So you came here to live with your brother. That makes sense. You know what they say about family—those are the folks that when you show up at the door, they *have* to take you in."

Vince silently congratulated Bob for finally saying something semi-intelligent.

Brad, who was ten years younger than Vince and a good deal heftier, came out of the kitchen, watched a moment, then sauntered toward them, wiping his hands on his still-clean apron. Brad wore kitchen whites and a tall chef's hat. Brad and Bob shook hands.

"This is my brother Brad. This is *Bob*."

"Your brother's a real comedian," said Bob.

Brad did not smile the way Bob did, a small fact for which Vince was grateful. "At moments," Brad said. "What are y'all up to?"

"Bob is here to sell me some insurance," Vince said. "I think we ought to get him a nice cold beer."

Bob held up a hand. "No thanks, not when I'm working. Glass of ice water'd be just fine."

"Insurance?" Brad asked.

"Yes. Since you wouldn't get ahold of someone to sell me some insurance, I got Randy, my ambulance driver, to do it. Now get *Bob* some water."

Bob opened his briefcase. "So, Randy tells me you've got a few medical problems."

"Randy ought to know. He's the one that drives me to dialysis three times a week. Then on top of two dried up kidneys, I got an ulcer, a heart condition, cataracts, high blood pressure, no left hip, and a broken arm that never healed right. And for the last year or two, I can't hear worth a good goddamn."

Bob had finally stopped smiling. "Sounds bad."

Brad was back in a moment with the water. He stood beside the booth rather than sit down.

"I want some life insurance," Vince said. "And I want to make this one here the beneficiary."

Brad began to fidget. "Vince, I don't like this."

"You don't have to like it, Little Brother. This is *my* decision."

Bob puffed himself up a bit, officious now that he was about to talk business. "I've got a few carriers here who insure terminally ill people." He took a handful of brochures from his briefcase and explained the costs and benefits of two policies to Vince, whose mind wandered to the cars stopped at the traffic light outside the restaurant.

"Whatever one you think is best," Vince said. "Just as long as you make this one here the beneficiary."

"There're a few questions on this form, if you don't mind," Bob said. "What's your occupation?"

"Retired. Short-order cook for twenty-two years. Tree surgeon and construction worker before that."

Bob's face brightened. "A cook?"

"So's this one," Vince said. "No. Excuse me. *I'm* the cook. This one's a *chef*. Means he gets paid more."

Bob smiled his blond, briefcase smile first toward Brad, then toward Vince. "So, I guess you two guys take turns doing the cooking at home, huh?"

"Hell no," Vince said. "You couldn't *pay* me to eat some of the god-awful stuff he makes. Have you ever heard of *Hay Two Fay* or some such abomination?"

"I *love* Cajun food," said Bob, his expression grave.

"And he's not exactly wild about the stuff I make," Vince continued. "I used to make the best meatloaf in Boston. Smothered beef and onions, New England boiled dinner. This one wouldn't eat it on a bet."

"This is very awkward, Vince," Brad said. "I feel like some kind of . . . mercenary."

"I'm gonna die. No shit. So make a dollar."

"It doesn't feel right."

"Don't be a moron." Vince turned back to Bob. "Now, how much is this little deal going to cost me?"

"It's not cheap," Bob said. "About a hundred and fifty dollars a month."

"I can handle that."

"Vince, for God's sake. Your social security only goes so far—"

"I can handle it, I said."

Brad shrugged. "Then you're not paying any more rent."

"Good. Now, tell me, *Bob*, how much will my charming brother here make?"

"Twenty-five hundred if you . . . er, pass on . . . the first year, six thousand if you go in the second year, and twenty thousand in the third year. And thereafter."

Vince sat back in his chair. "By third year, you mean I just have to live two more years and then one day?"

"Yessir."

Vince nodded. "I'll give it a shot. Where do I sign?"

AFTER BOB LEFT, Brad paced the room. "This isn't right," he said.

"Why the hell not? I didn't have much reason to live a few minutes ago. Now I do. I think we ought to celebrate. Didn't you say some store around here sells live Maine lobsters? I could go for a lobster. Dipped in melted butter. Like we used to eat them back home. Strawberry shortcake for dessert."

"Fat and cholesterol to clog your arteries even worse, possibly give you another stroke. No doubt a major one this time. An overload of protein to raise hell with your non-functioning kidneys."

"I go on the machine in two days."

"You'll suffer until then."

"I ain't suffered in hours. I'm ready."

"Lobsters are really expensive down here."

"That don't bother me a god damned bit," Vince said, smiling for the first time. "You're the one who's paying."

Brad threw up his arms. "This is a perfect example of what makes me so uncomfortable about this. I buy you a lobster, you have a heart attack, and some court decides that I tried to kill you to get the insurance money."

Vince clicked his dentures and said nothing. He hadn't thought of that angle. "Look, I'm just trying to thank you for taking me in and taking care of me instead of putting me in a nursing home. You're a bachelor now. You ought to have that apartment to yourself so you could bring girlfriends over without them having to listen to me throwing up or—"

"I don't *mind* taking care of you. You'd do the same. Now you make it seem like I'm supposed to get paid for it."

In the pause, Vince considered once again how much Brad was a worrier, like their mother. Brad had their father's face, but with all that weight he'd put on since his divorce, he had their mother's body. The weight somehow made Brad look younger, stretching out his post-divorce wrinkles, while Vince looked a lot older than his fifty-two years. People took them for father and son rather than brothers.

"So, are you telling me *no* lobster?" Vince could see that Brad was shaking his head, but not in a way that meant no. "I ain't had a Maine lobster in five, six years."

"I thought you swore you'd never eat a lobster south of Massachusetts."

"I take it back."

Brad wheeled Vince into the kitchen and told his crew he was taking the night off. "Sammy knows what to do, and he'll be here in an hour. If Mr. Caro shows up, tell him I had a family emergency."

"Have fun," one of the black kitchen helpers said. Vince made Brad stop the wheelchair. Grabbing Mary behind her head, Vince pulled the woman's broad, glistening face down to his own and kissed her mouth before she could protest. Mary's open eyes grew wider, and she even let out a low moan, but she didn't rear back.

Brad squeezed Vince's shoulder hard. "Vince! For Christ's sake!"

Mary broke the embrace and stood up, smiling. "Let him be. He's *good*. Got a tongue big as a toy truck."

IT WAS A Japanese car. Vince tried not to think about it as Brad guided him in. Vince had made it a point *not* to get used to riding in the Toyota and frequently urged Brad to buy himself a good, second-hand Caddy. Vince offered to put up half the money. But Brad didn't care what he drove, Vince could see. He had no pride.

While Brad folded up the wheelchair and wrestled it into the trunk, Vince thought about the grocery store they were going to and how he still enjoyed looking at all the shelves of food, whether he could eat any of it or not, or even see it very clearly.

They drove.

"Well, Little Brother. Looks like you finally have yourself a *real* investment. After you lost all that money on the stock market."

"You're kind of crude sometimes. You know that?"

"I try." They had always been different. Vince wanted to stay in the army but their mother made him come home after their father died. Brad couldn't get out of the army fast enough, after they snared him for 'Nam and he spent a year as a finance clerk in an air-conditioned office in Bangkok. And whereas Vince flunked out of high school, Brad had an MBA and a diploma from a chef school over in Atlanta.

"How you gonna cook your lobster?" Vince asked.

"I guess I'll boil it. Melt some butter."

"Ha! I figured that'd be too simple for you."

"Then maybe I'll stir-fry it with snow peas and sliced ginger root."

"Sounds more like you." Vince felt an ease of heart that he recognized as a distinct departure from his usual frame of mind. For the first time in years, he knew he'd done a good thing. He'd seen enough terminal cases at the dialysis center in San Bernadino to know just how bad he might get before he kicked off. Brad had no idea what they were in for.

"This insurance thing still bothers me," Brad said. "I can't help but feel that something's going on here. Besides pure generosity."

"Just expressing my gratitude, Little Brother. For all the little things you've done for me over the years." Vince paused. "Like throwing me out of Birmingham five years ago. Having my lights and gas shut off and letting the landlord over at that roach motel I was staying in throw me out. And letting the cops haul me off for breaking that window at your place. Little things like that."

"Vince, I . . ."

"Don't apologize. That's what I'm trying to tell you; I don't drink no more. Partly because of you. Mostly because I can't keep water down now, let alone booze."

As the Toyota slid through suburbia toward the grocery store, Vince took note of every car they passed, assessing the worthiness of each driver to have functioning kidneys, efficient enzymes, crisp eyesight.

"I used to hate you for taking me in and putting up with me. You were just too goddam pious to be true, weren't you?"

"So this insurance thing is supposed to be some kind of punishment that you—"

"It wasn't until you put my ass out, wheelchair and all, that I started respecting you. The big lesson we all have to face sooner or later is how to live a life. Yours, or someone else's. I was never that good at living mine, and you were never as good as you thought at living yours."

Brad smiled, recognizing once again Vince's ability to summon high-level insight at unexpected moments. He thought about all the left-footed ways Vince had tried to be a big brother to him over the years—a role model, as Vince once put it, his life of alcoholic dissolution notwithstanding. One instance in particular came to mind. It was the summer when Vince was working as a salad chef down on Route One toward Old Orchard Beach. He got Brad on as his *assistant* salad chef, although Brad was really more of a dishwasher than anything. Vince tried to appear a lot more important than he was, strutting and mumbling around the kitchen as he inspected things. When one of the waitresses, who happened to be a real bitch, complained that Vince was putting too much dressing on the salad he was making for her, Vince asked her if she wanted to serve the salad or wear it. "I'll *wear* it, if you're man enough," she said. So Vince threw the salad at her. She ran shrieking out of the kitchen, the pink salad dressing streaming down her black hair and rouged face. Vince motioned to Brad and headed toward the back door, untying his apron and letting it drop on the floor. Brad took the cue and did the same.

"Don't take any shit from none of these sanctimonious bastards," Vince said proudly as they waited to cross the honking, hollering four-lane road of nighttime convertibles to find a pay phone and call their mother to come pick them up. "I don't."

Expense Report

YE OLDE Beefeater Tavern was a cut-stone basement room under a once gracious three-story apartment building that faced a busy street. The restaurant's patio entrance was in the alley out back. Inside, the stone walls were hung with shields and swords and coats of arms, and flickering candle lanterns. The Beefeater was considered a bit pricey for ordinary dinner outings, but it was a favorite spot for special occasions. Tonight was such an occasion for a select group: Red Bean Raoul Renault was back in town, and it was expense account time. His party of twelve raucously bunched through the doorway just after five-thirty. Their chairs scraped on the brick floor, rasping against all the laughter as they sat. Red Bean sold type out of New Orleans to ten or twenty—he wasn't exactly sure how many—ad agency art directors in places like Montgomery, Memphis, Birmingham.

Red Bean took his usual place at the head of the table.

"You may wonder why I've gathered us here tonight," he said, his black-mustachioed smile spreading like the smoke from the lanterns. "It's because we in New Orleans have decided to go on a hunger strike," now he allowed himself to appeared heated, "until you people here in Birmingham buy more fucking *type!*"

"Hear, hear," they answered, their glasses raised and clinking. All of Red Bean's favorite Birmingham people were there: Still Jill, Ivan the Terrible Copywriter, Gina the Greek, Evelyne the Mountain Cajun Viking. It was a typical Red Bean Raoul table; everyone was at least sociably drunk, if not considerably more.

The only thing amiss was that plans for after dinner activities were not yet settled. All the way up from New Orleans that afternoon Red Bean had been thinking about Still Jill and her short, black, curled-under hair, her slender fingers and light blue nails, her small breasts and rounded bottom. But Jill, whose real name was Norma, seemed utterly engrossed, perhaps even in love, with Ivan the Terrible Copywriter. A few weeks earlier, Norma had come to visit Red Bean in New Orleans and stayed the weekend with him. In the darkness of his barren bedroom in the warehouse district, she confided that in seventh grade she used to fantasize that she was a cheerleader named Jill. That was what Red Bean had called her ever since whenever he phoned.

If he couldn't have her tonight, at least he approved of Ivan.

The appetizers arrived. Red Bean smiled a little sadly, like a man without a date, at the bounty of baby spare ribs, stuffed mushrooms, baked tomatoes and feta cheese, escargot, fried mozzarella. The river of food seemed unending, and it made Red Bean think he detected a familiar frenzied level of joking that had, in the past, meant lots of business from his table. It was time to forge ahead with an unmistakable show of good will on the part of TypiCal, Inc., the Crescent City's showcase of the typographic arts, as Red Bean billed his and Warren's shop.

"Listen up, friends," Red Bean announced. "I couldn't help but notice the list of exquisite wines offered by this superb establishment. Perhaps we should allow our resident wine connoisseur, Mr. Ivan the Terrible Copywriter, to light our way to some wine worthy of our attention instead of this pink formaldehyde that has insinuated itself onto our far more worthy palates."

"Hear, hear," said the new guy, Marvin, a dapper young black man who had been a cartographer in the Army before joining the creative staff at Axel and Arden. Red Bean had given Marvin the name Paint, the Patron Saint of bad clip art.

"Hear, hear," said Still Jill into her glass as she emptied it.

"Yes," said Ivan, raising his eyebrows and picking up the wine list that Red Bean had nudged across the table.

"Don't hurt me too bad, brother," Red Bean whispered.

Ivan raised his eyebrows. "Backing down already?"

"We *are* on hunger strike in New Orleans. I think I mentioned that."

"We could try this 1974 Martha's Vineyard," said Ivan.

"They make wine in Massachusetts?"

"California. Stag's Leap."

"Don't confuse me. How much is it?"

"Seventy-two dollars a bottle. Four bottles should do it, wouldn't you say?"

"How much type will you buy from me?"

"For a bottle of 1974 Martha's Vineyard, I'd probably buy all my type from you for the next two weeks."

"And would that, by chance, be two hundred and fifty dollars' worth of type?"

"I'm only writing one headline this month, actually. I'm copy chief now. I just supervise people."

"How many words in your headline?"

"I dunno. Ten?"

"Thirty dollars a word. Sounds about right for superior typography. And if you supervise everybody, why the hell aren't you sending them to me for their type?"

"I just do headlines. Talk to Gina. Or Evelyne. Or Mildred. Or— what is it you call her—*Still* Jill?" Ivan arched his left eyebrow to a new height.

"Gentlemen don't tell," said Red Bean.

"And ladies don't move much?"

TO RED BEAN'S relief, the salads began to arrive. He needed the distraction from his datelessness. The bread baskets had once more erupted with every imaginable shape of roll, and Red Bean could not stop himself from squeezing one roll that most looked like a small, firm breast. No Still Jill tonight. Or perhaps any night.

There was always Morbid Mildred, who designed ads for Birmingham's biggest funeral home and cemetery. She was dark-haired, purposely dour, and wore black blouses or dresses that opened generously over her shoulders and cleavage. Although Red Bean had never been with Morbid Mildred, he had at times thought she seemed interested in him. Mildred was a big-time coker; she'd already visited the ladies' room three times and come back sniffling each time.

Red Bean would have preferred blond little Gina the Greek, but Gina also appeared taken for the night. She had brought a man whom Red Bean had never met. He was tall and graying and somber-mannered, although the gray seemed premature and temporary, as if a good night's sleep could have cured him. He was also the only one at the table other than Red Bean who wore a suit. Red Bean tried to remember the guy's name. Tom; that was it. And Tom wasn't having a good time. Gina seemed uneasy whenever she looked at Tom.

"So, what do you do, Tom?" Red Bean asked.

"Nothing."

"Ah, my own ambition in life. Do you give lessons?"

"No." Tom's blank eyes wandered around the restaurant, stopping at the far end of the table where his gaze fixed itself on the flamboyantly redheaded Evelyne Boudreaux, the Mountain Cajun Viking, who sat next to Paint. Evelyne's wavy hair gushed from her head and down over her shoulders and breasts. She wore a white summer dress that was cut low in the neck line, and she glistened with rings, bracelets, earrings, and a sequined headband. In the candle-lit corner where she sat, Evelyne sparkled with every laugh and toss of her head. Tom rose from his chair and stood at his place, his eyes craning toward Evelyne. Everyone stopped laughing and watched. Evelyne seemed to shrink between her suddenly hunched shoulders.

Red Bean buried his discomfort in his smile. Tom was bigger, at least five years younger, and seemed to have a certain quiet strength that Red Bean had sensed in the few truly deranged people he had known.

"This could be a very nice restaurant," Tom said, his eyes roaming the room absently. "I always wanted to own a restaurant like this."

"It's never too late," Red Bean said. "Sit down and let's talk about it."

But Tom did not sit down. Instead, he buttoned his suit coat and walked slowly toward another table.

"Who is this guy?" Red Bean whispered to Gina.

"He was an old boyfriend of mine. Back in high school. I haven't seen him in ten years. He called this afternoon and wanted to take me out for drinks. He sounded so damned depressed. I didn't think you'd mind if I brought him."

"For Christ's sake, I was hoping to see you tonight."

"Don't let me forget," Gina whispered back. "He asked me to make sure he takes his medication."

They listened, surprised by his sudden amiability as Tom spoke to the six middle-aged people at the next table.

"How is everyone tonight?" Tom asked.

"Fine," said one man. "Fine," said another.

"Good. Let us know if you need anything." Tom's face became blank again as he wandered toward another table.

"He's nuts," said Red Bean.

"Nuts," repeated Gina the Greek, Paint, Still Jill, Ivan the Terrible Copywriter, and Evelyne the Mountain Cajun Viking. "Nuts or no nuts," winked Morbid Mildred, who had returned from another visit to the ladies' room. "He's kind of cute. In fact, he's quite handsome."

"He's all yours," Gina said.

THE ENTREES began to arrive. Red Bean raked in the aromas of osso buco, prime rib, teriyaki shark, veal picatta. Horrified by the prices or not, Red Bean considered, his boss Warren would have approved of the place. It was ironic that Warren had picked this week for his annual retreat at the Benedictine monastery in Cullman, less than an hour north of Birmingham. Red Bean was now seized by the image of Warren on his knees, praying himself into a sweat in the unair-conditioned stone cell where he allowed himself to be locked and deprived of food for forty-eight straight hours each year. Red Bean had even used the idea for his last Mardi Gras costume, dressing as Warren on retreat in a ragged brown robe, kneeling on styrofoam packing peanuts (Warren knelt on raw rice) in a large, red, top-of-the-line toy wagon, towed by Ivan, who had come to New Orleans for the festivities, along with twenty-three of Red Bean's other business contacts. Twenty-three carpet campers was nothing, Red Bean had thought at the time. In 1988 he'd had a record thirty-six. That was the year he'd borrowed some stolen vestments from a former seminarian friend of his and marched in the parade as Pope John-Paul-George-and-Ringo. The year before that he was the blind gynecologist and Ivan was his seeing-eye dog.

The table had finished the Martha's Vineyard, and Ivan had moved them along to a Mondavi Reserve. Red Bean tried to recall whether or not he'd actually gotten a taste of that Martha's Vineyard production, and whether anyone, most of all the infamous Ivan the Terrible Copywriter, had bothered to thank him for it.

TOM REAPPEARED, holding open the kitchen door for two waiters with serving trays perched on their shoulders. Tom came and sat down beside Gina. The table fell to silence, except for Morbid Mildred's intermittent sniffling.

Tom's eyes wistfully swept over the table. "Who's paying for this?"

"My typography shop in New Orleans is paying for it."

"I figured as much."

"Why do you ask?"

"I ordered some champagne. I didn't think you'd mind."

"How kind of you. Was it the Cordon Negro or the Dom Perignon?"

"The expensive stuff."

Red Bean felt his blood pound a little harder, but he kept his amiable, unblinking smile on low beam and studied Tom's bland stare. "Don't you think that was just a wee bit presumptuous?"

Tom the Zombie shrugged. "I just figured this is what people like you do."

Red Bean forced himself to smile another moment at Tom before he went to cancel the champagne order, but at that moment the kitchen doors bulged open, and the wine steward wheeled out a cart with ten teetering bottles of champagne, already uncorked.

Red Bean decided that rather than invite Tom the Zombie outside to beat the shit out of him, he should try one last stab at diplomacy. He leaned toward Tom's ear and whispered, "Do you think that at anytime in your life you will, for whatever reason, have occasion to buy type?"

"Sure," Tom said, also lowering his voice, but at the same time coming to life more than he had all night. He leaned close to Red Bean and his lips parted in a near-smile. "You can do my menus, I just bought this place."

Without hesitation, Red Bean flashed the warmest version of his smile. "Congratulations, brother."

"I'm not your brother."

"Neither is my brother," said Red Bean. "I hear he's my sister."

Tom wandered off among the customers again. The notion that Tom had not really bought the place flitted at the edge of Red Bean's wine-warmed mind, but he dismissed his thought as typical paranoia. There was some unnameable thing about Tom the Zombie that did seem rich. Red Bean told himself he had suspected it all along.

NOT LONG AFTER Tom disappeared, the wine steward wheeled out another cart of champagne, but he headed for a different table. Red Bean felt only a moment of relief—until the wine steward pointed toward him, and several people at the table raised their champagne flutes and nodded their thanks.

Red Bean raised his own glass and smiled back.

Four waiters collected the plates from the table while two others brought fruits and cheeses and yogurt. Everyone wanted desert, so the waiters trooped out once again with sorbets and mousses and streudels. Then it was time for liquers. The conversation had revived itself almost from the moment when Tom wandered off, but Red Bean sulked in silence as he watched Gina the Greek finally laughing and talking with the others, ignoring him.

"Oh my god!" said Gina. "Where's Tom? I forgot all about his medication."

"I saw him out in the parking lot awhile ago," said Morbid Mildred, giggling. "I gave him some of *my* medication. And then he drove off."

"Oh my *god!*" Gina said again, her face pale and stiff with horror.

"My *car*! I had his medication so he wouldn't forget it, and he had my wallet and keys so I wouldn't have to carry a purse."

"Do you know where he lives?" Red Bean asked, trying to appear calm and stolid for Gina.

"Hell no. I haven't seen him since the senior prom."

"Was he rich back then?"

"Not that I know of."

"Is he rich now? Rich enough to buy this restaurant?"

Gina shook her head. "I have no idea."

Red Bean hailed the next waiter who passed the table. "Bring me the check please."

The tab came to well over a thousand dollars. Grace under pressure, Red Bean told himself. His hand quivered as he signed the credit card slip. Everyone except Paint had gone out to the parking lot to see if Gina's car was back.

"Thanks, man," Paint said. "I've got a little brochure job I can send you in a week or two."

"Please do. Tell Miss Gina I'll be out in a minute to drive her home."

Alone at the table as he waited for his copy of the credit card slip, Red Bean surveyed the carnage for the first time. A thousand dollars. Warren would first turn purple, then yellowish, then he'd fire Red Bean again. Although they were legally partners, they had long ago recognized that the shop needed a head man, and that Raoul would be a poor choice for the job.

The old maitre-d' limped toward the table, his concave temples twitching. "I'm terribly sorry sir, but the limit on this card is five hundred dollars."

Warren, you son of a bitch, Red Bean thought. It was a new credit card, and Red Bean had forgotten to ask about the limit. Red Bean gave the maitre-d' his most confidence-sharing smile. "I do know the new owner. I'm sure he'd—"

"New owner, sir?"

Red Bean searched through his pockets for other credit cards. He knew the American Express was unusable, since he'd forgotten to make the payment this month. His Visa was much too close to the limit to absorb a thousand dollars.

"I don't suppose you'd take an out-of-town check?"

The maitre-d's face sucked itself drier and whiter. "We do not take even local checks."

"I'll get another credit card out of my car."

"I will accompany you."

He'd just take up a collection from his friends, Red Bean decided, and try to pay everyone back once he got home. But when they went outside, Red Bean saw that everyone had already left. Only his own little white economy rental car sat there under the anticrime street light.

The maitre-d' sighed. "I must ask you to come inside the restaurant while I call the police."

Red Bean smiled. "I understand completely. May I put a slightly long-distance telephone call on my tab?"

RED BEAN PACED on the leash of the three-foot telephone cord. He wanted to smoke, but he refused to ask anyone for a cigarette. He wished he'd snorted a line of coke with Morbid Mildred when she'd offered it, or had the joint he'd almost brought from home. But no, he was trying to behave himself on this trip.

"Sir? Mr. Forest says he doesn't want to talk to you. He said there are no emergencies he cares to take part in tonight, and that you're not to disturb him while he's on retreat."

Red Bean could contain his rage no longer. "Tell that hypocritical, duplicitous, sadistic son of a bitch to get his ass to this phone!"

The silence lasted several moments before the line went dead. As Red Bean hung up the phone, it all became clear. Warren had scheduled his retreat to coincide with Red Bean's trip to Birmingham. "I told you never to spend more than five hundred dollars on *any* trip ever, ever, ever," he could hear Warren say two days from now when he would drive down from the monastery in Cullman to spring his old college buddy from jail.

Two police officers walked in before Red Bean Raoul had time even to shrug, which was the closest he could come to an explanation.

Perfect Greek

DENNIS HAD noticed that Sylvie was one person at home and another at The Greek Garden Restaurant, where she worked as head waitress and self-anointed tyrant. The part of her job that she seemed to like best was firing the waitresses she supervised. She had many times declared that she would never hire a black waitress, whether Wallace had let that one into the university or not. That was Tuscaloosa; this was Bayou La Batre.

Sylvie was tall, erect, and able to summon a metallic stare. With her hive of red hair, weighty cobalt eyelids and dangerously long lashes, she looked like the bowsprit of an acient ship. But when she was working extra hours to fill in for her latest casualty, her face would light up in an ocean of smile as she raked the tips off the counter and tables.

At home, Sylvie was anything but a despot, sweeping about the apartment in her bathrobe and hair curlers, self-consciously trying to repress her toothless smile as a cloud of cigarette smoke followed her like a windblown scarf. She freely handed out money to Elmer and Lorraine, her teenaged kids, who pocketed the unrequested money without seeming to notice the hand that held it out to them. At the restaurant Sylvie took delight in complaining about how much the kids cost her, and how irrevocably she had spoiled them, allowing Elmer to smoke openly since his fourteenth birthday, and more or less insisting that Lorraine buy any magazine, record, or blouse the girl had so much as pointed at in a store window. She made her show of complaint mainly to Dennis, Elmer's best friend, who worked as dishwasher Tuesday nights at The Greek Garden. Sylvie gave Dennis the job after Elmer refused it.

"Old Lard-ass don't know it yet," Sylvie told Dennis as they drank coffee together in the kitchen Dennis's first night at The Greek Garden, "but the gravy train is fixing to derail." She'd been singing the same song for a month.

George Kollias, the owner, waddled into the kitchen, the end of his long necktie tucked inside the waist of his pants. Given a new audience, Sylvie turned her tirade on the boss.

"All that lard-ass teenager of mine wants to do is diddle his girlfriend and watch TV all day."

But George Kollias didn't care what was going on in Sylvie's life, or anyone else's. Every day when George came in, he drew a cup of coffee and went to sit in the last booth, where he loaded the juke box selector with quarters, punched up an hour-long stream of Ray Charles and Brenda Lee, and pored over the Greek newspaper that came out each Wednesday—and reread the old one every afternoon until the new one came out. During the mealtime rush he stood at the register and took cash, but George did little else. The only person to whom he spoke much was Dennis, whom he had taught to cuss in Greek, claiming that Dennis had a perfect Greek accent.

"You got Greek blood in you somewhere," George insisted.

"Irish and Cajun," Dennis replied.

He'd lead Dennis by the arm and point out a booth of gray-haired male customers who had driven down to Bayou La Batre from Mobile, or from Malbis, across the bay.

"Go over there," George said, "and say I sent a message; tell them I said they're all a bunch of *muni lifti*. Say it."

"Muni lifti."

"Perfect. *Perfect*. And you not even Greek."

"What's it mean?"

"Don't worry about that, just go tell them."

Dennis would deliver the message, the three or four old men would roar and slap the table, and Dennis, sensing that he should feel embarrassed, would clear their dishes and saunter back to the kitchen.

George would holler, "He speak *perfect* Greek, huh?"

THE ONLY member of the staff who was immune to Sylvie's tyranny was Uncle Andros, a round-faced, jovial old man in big, black-framed glasses who had come to America only two years earlier. He was not the head cook, only the setup cook since he didn't know enough English to understand the orders from the waitresses. But most of the customers thought Uncle Andros was the head cook, since he was George's relative and the only one who wore a chef's hat. In spite of his struggle with the language, Uncle Andros did know enough English to tell Dennis, "Don't talk that trash," whenever George taught Dennis another vulgar expression. Uncle Andros would scold George in a tumble of angry, rapid syllables that sent George shuffling out of the kitchen, clucking his quiet laugh.

"You learn *good* Greek," Uncle Andros told Dennis. And the old man would make Dennis repeat a line from Homer or Plato. Dennis ate well on the nights when he worked; George rewarded his perfect vulgarity with fried peach pie, and Andros rewarded Dennis's perfect lines from *The Odessey* with fried oysters, or an icy glass cup of shrimp cocktail, or a batch of beignets that Andros would make just for Dennis.

Dennis was eating a fried apple pie drenched in melting ice cream when Sylvie came into the after-dinner kitchen carrying two cups of coffee. "You're the first dishwasher I ever saw George like," Sylvie said. "He's always telling me you got ambition. He says it every time you're here." The roar of the fan and the splashing of the dishwashing machine made the kitchen sound like a monsoon. Sylvie grimaced at it. "Shut at least one a them damned things off. I want to talk to you."

Dennis flicked the washer's off switch, leaving only the breezy gasp of the fan.

"What do you think of Lily, you like her? Or do you think Lard-ass could do better?"

"She's okay."

"You think she's cute?"

"She's okay."

Dennis knew the next question by heart. He considered it a game that he most easily won with silence.

"Do you think he's diddling her?" Sylvie asked, her voice rising in a foolish giggle. Dennis figured she giggled whenever she asked him questions like that because she didn't really want to know but she felt a curious obligation to ask. Dennis blew on his coffee. He felt her eyes and finally had to look up and smile.

"What?" he asked.

"Tell me what them two are up to."

"How should I know?"

"He tells you everything. I know the way boys are."

Then Sylvie said nothing for a few moments. With the door open, the kitchen smelled of the low tide in the channel and the garbage cans in the alley. Sylvie held her nose and pointed. "Shut that goddam door."

Dennis closed the door and went back to the sink, where he drew water to wash the last two vats from the steam table. She lit a cigarette and blew the smoke toward the ceiling. "Them two remind me of the way I was when I was a teenager. God, my mother drove me nuts."

"Yeah?" The pots thumped in the sink as Dennis scoured.

"I had a boyfriend named Frank, and me and him went together for about six months when I was a sophomore. We'd sit in the living room necking and my mother used to sneak up behind us and smack him on the side of the head if she didn't like where he had his hands."

"Why didn't you go someplace where you could be alone?"

Sylvie tossed her head with a laugh. "Mama wouldn't let me out of sight. She didn't want to let me out of the house for the whole four years the war was going on."

"Why not?"

"Too many sailors. Port city. Lots of cute sailors. Ten cute sailors for every teenage girl in Mobile." Sylvie thrust her massive chest forward. "All the sailors stared at me. I never could figure out why."

Dennis grinned.

"Lorraine's gonna be built, too," Sylvie went on. "Just like me. She'll be a good girlfriend for you in two or three years. You watch."

Dennis already knew all he wanted to about Lorraine, but he said nothing. He sometimes thought about Lorraine's large, full breasts, but he also thought about her hooked nose and small, puffy, unmade-up eyes that too closely resembled her mother's.

Sylvie was looking at the school books Dennis had brought to work with him. "Latin and algebra," she said sympathetically. "I wish Lard-ass had a tenth the ambition you have. But all he ever thinks about anymore is Lily."

Dennis tried to look busy washing the pots, but he felt her eyes.

"I wish to hell you'd level with me. I'm his mother. I have a right to know so I can be ready for the worst."

Dennis sighed. "What if he asked me about you? And your policeman friend, Ted? How would you feel about my telling him what I know?"

Sylvie's smile closed down. "I *knew* I shouldn't'a told you about that." Although she didn't move, her being shrank back from him. She threw her cigarette on the floor and stepped on it. "I don't want him making me a grandmother at thirty-five."

Dennis shrugged. "If he does, that was his choice, not yours."

Now she was angry. "You call thinking with your little head *choosing?*" The silence lasted. Dennis expected her to stomp out of the kitchen, or fire him. Or both. He didn't care at the moment if she fired him, but he did feel bad about making her angry.

"I haven't told a soul about Ted," he said.

"You better not."

Dennis thought about the way Sylvie acted whenever Ted came into the restaurant. Ted was tall and thin and haunted-looking. Dennis felt sure that Ted had probably committed a few crimes as bad as those for which he arrested people. Dennis had never seen Ted crack the smallest grin, and yet Sylvie claimed that he was lots of fun to be with. Dennis knew about Sylvie's other affairs, too. Everyone at The Greek Garden, customers and employees alike, knew about Sylvie's affairs. Max the cabbie, for instance, whom Dennis considered to be only one evolutionary step above a grave maggot. It pained Dennis to see Sylvie talking to Max. Ted seemed plenty weird, but it was possible that Ted had done a noble thing or two in his career as a cop. Max the cabbie, on the other hand, was not noble; he was just a stubble-faced scum who drove the hookers around the airport and the bars up in Mobile looking for tricks. It was said that Max let his mother die of a heart attack rather than take her to the hospital so he could collect her insurance. But someone else, it turned out, was the beneficiary.

"What are you thinking about?" Sylvie asked.

"Nothing."

"You don't look too happy."

Dennis rinsed the last pot, shut off the faucet, and dried his hands on his apron. He remembered his cup of coffee on the counter. "Forget about Elmer," Dennis said. "Tell me something new about you." He watched her closely, wondering how she'd take it if he asked her why she fooled around with someone as slimey as Max the cabbie. But Dennis had already decided he didn't want to know what she saw in Max for fear that whatever it was could permanently damage his view of her. Like something to do with her ability to throw money at her kids.

"You got enough on me already," she said, not quite smiling but no longer glaring either.

"I want more. Tell me . . . tell me . . . about the first time you—you know—*got* it."

A high blush came over her face, heightening the garish makeup, and Dennis was amused to see that he had the power to embarrass her.

"I can't do that," she said.

"You said once you could tell me anything."

Her eyes narrowed. "Only if you tell me what Lard-ass and Lily are up to."

"Was it that guy Frank you mentioned a minute ago?"

"No. Johnny. And I ain't telling you nothing about it."

"Ah, Johnny. I should have known he had a fancy name. And what was he like?"

"Short. Rugged. Dark-haired. Forget it."

"Was he nice?"

She sighed. Dennis saw that she was already remembering details. "Yeah, I guess you could say Johnny was nice. He had a real sweet smile."

"Aha. A sweet smile . . ."

She looked into her coffee again. "He was Italian. He had a dog named Luigi."

Dennis waited a moment before trying to restart her. "By the way, how old were you when this happened?"

"Oh, fourteen or fifteen."

"Hmmmm. The curious stage."

"I didn't even know enough to be curious. Mama never told us kids nothing about that part of life."

"But didn't you have, you know, *feelings* that made you wonder?"

"I dunno. I can't remember."

"Okay, so you were fifteen. Or maybe fourteen. Now, were you in love with this Johnny?"

"No. Not then. I didn't even know him then."

"Interesting. Then how did you happen to go to bed with him if you didn't know him?"

"He was my best friend's brother. But he was older than us. He never paid no attention to us kids."

"What made him suddenly pay attention?"

Sylvie stood up straight and thrust out her chest again. "I can't imagine," she said, laughing.

"Okay. But I'm puzzled. You weren't in love, you didn't even know the guy. You weren't particularly curious. It doesn't make any sense so far."

"I've told you too much already." She took a long sip to finish her coffee, then set the empty cup on the sideboard with Dennis's other dirty dishes. "I've got work to do." But Sylvie made no move to go out front and instead lit another cigarette. Dennis noticed that her eyes were cloudy.

"It was the weekend before he was supposed to go off in the army, and I happened to be staying overnight at Nita's house. The second night I was there, he came into the room where Nita and me was sleeping and told Nita to go sleep in his room. He never said nothing about why or any of that. So she got up and left, and he crawled into the bed with me."

"Did you ask him just what the hell he was doing?"

"No."

"Did he kiss you and stuff?"

"Oh, yeah . . ."

"Did you tell him no when he tried to do more than just kiss you?"

"I didn't really have time to. It happened so fast."

Why can't I find a girl like that, thought Dennis. "Did you like what he was doing to you?"

She shrugged. "I didn't like it and I didn't dislike it. I didn't really know what to think of it."

"Come on . . ."

"I'm serious. Mama didn't tell us girls nothing. I had no idea what he was up to until after it was all over and I told one of my girlfriends about it."

"And what did your girlfriend say?"

Sylvie finally laughed. "She said I was going to hell."

Dennis shook his head. "Amazing. So, did it excite you at all?"

"A little. It was different."

"Did he give you that cute smile you said he had while he was doing it to you?"

"What are you asking me about this stuff for?"

"I'm curious. I want to learn everything I can about how these things happen. Now, at what point did you realize that there was something strange going on here?"

Sylvie chuckled. "I ain't figured it out yet."

Dennis tried to imagine Sylvie at fifteen, but he could only picture her as a slightly smaller version of the Sylvie at home in her housecoat and curlers, or the Sylvie at work with her makeup and uniform and starched hair. Then the image turned into Lorraine, but Dennis knew that Lorraine was very different from Sylvie, no matter how strong their physical similarity. Lorraine was passive, humorless, more interested in stamp-collecting than boys, even at fifteen. She didn't breathe hard or even seem to notice anything the one time when Dennis fondled her breasts; she just stared.

"So then what?" he asked.

Sylvie mimicked him. "So then what? So then next day he left."

"Huh. Did he ever write to you?"

"Oh sure. He sent me a Christmas card one time."

"And did you write back to him?"

"Hah! Me? Write a letter? At fourteen? I doubt it."

"And did you ever see him again?"

"Well . . . no. Johnny got killed. In the Phillipines."

"Did you feel bad when you heard about it?"

Her eyes were misty again when she reached over and pinched Dennis's arm. "Of course I felt bad. I didn't hear about it until the war was almost over. Nita and me ended up at different high schools and we didn't see much of each other. By the time I heard about Johnny, I was already pregnant and married."

Sylvie stared at the steam table. Dennis imagined that she was thinking about what it might have been like to marry Johnny instead of Elmer Senior, and to have had lithe, olive-skinned children with thick, Mediterranean eyebrows and black hair, instead of two blond stumps. Maybe she would have been something better than a waitress. Or something worse.

She looked at him again and her eyes were pink around the edges, but Dennis could see that she was not going to cry; she'd already moved beyond that point to the stage of a quivering smile.

"I don't know why I'm telling you these things."

George waddled into the kitchen carrying a sliver of pecan pie, which he held off to his side. "Say SKA-TAH."

"SKA-TAH."

"Perfect. Here's your pie."

Uncle Andros burst through the swinging kitchen door, scowling first at George, then at Dennis.

"Sing in me, Muse, and make me tell the story."

"Sing in me, Muse . . ." But he couldn't remember the rest of it.

Sylvie stamped her foot. "Tell me, damn you. Is he screwing her or not?"

Smoking Section

WHENEVER Melba wanted to discuss a sensitive topic with Bickford, she suggested that they go out to eat. In a public place, she surmised, Bickford could not go fully ballistic if he got angry. Her favorite place to argue was Romeo's, where they had been eating at least once a month for most of the four years they had been married. It was a second marriage for both. Neither had children, although Bick sometimes said he'd like to have one. But Melba felt that her biological clock had stopped ticking at least five years ago, and Bick was so precise in his recurring description of the child they would have—an exceptionally good-looking girl with rich red hair who would be both artistically and scientifically inclined—that she knew he wasn't serious about it.

Melba, after all, had black hair that she wore in a twist, and thin brows. She was reasonably trim in her figure, as she felt was expected of her, but she was trim in a shapeless way. And Bick, whose remaining hair was also black, had been thin, gaunt even, until only a few weeks ago, when he abruptly began to bloat up. He had not yet admitted this to his wardrobe; he thought that by keeping his coat unbuttoned, he would avoid anyone's noticing how badly his clothes fit him, even though he suspected that, like him, everyone could feel the sleeves of his suit coats getting shorter by the day as the edges crept up his wrists. The chances of their producing an exceptionally pretty redheaded girl child were remote.

From the restaurant's street-level entrance, Bick and Mel descended the steps to a landing from which they could see the dimly lighted dining room with its red and white checkered, plastic table cloths and candles burning in straw-wrapped wine bottles. Booths lined the rose-colored, paint-peeling walls, and four small tables filled the area between the two rows of booths. Faded, rain-stained posters of Naples Bay and the Grand Canal of Venice and the armless, crumbling ruins of various statues against perfectly blue skies clung loosely to the walls. Frank Sinatra sang "Strangers in the Night" from a scratchy record on an old stereo console in the darkest corner.

Johnny and Lester Romeo worked out front, and their mother, Angel, ran the kitchen. Johnny, who went to college during the day, was strictly a sports fan. He talked up football and basketball to everyone who sat at his tables. Lester, who had finished college several years earlier, liked to talk about art and politics with his customers. Lester's hair was glisteny dark and curly, thinning already at the crown.

And Angel Romeo, whose facial creases seemed to deepen with each new night she spent in the hot kitchen, did as little talking as possible, as if she were trying to conserve her energy for her work. You had to pass through the kitchen to get to the restrooms, and Angel (she had dropped the final *a* from her name when she was in high school in the 1950s) seldom looked up from the busy stove. Six or seven fans blew at her from all directions, hardly budging a single gray curl under her tight hair net.

Tonight, when Lester saw Bickford and Melba coming down the stairs, he pointed toward a booth. Bick stopped, shook his head toward Lester, and touched Melba's arm.

"I don't want to sit there."

"Why not?"

"I want to sit in the smoking section."

Her face wrinkled in a bemused frown. "Why?"

"Because I want to smoke."

"Since when do you smoke?"

"Almost five years."

Melba let her mouth fall open. "Five years? You've been smoking since I *met* you?"

Bick took her arm and led her to the last booth. Lester brought wine glasses and the usual bottle of Chianti Classico Riserva.

"Bick. Mel. Are we slumming tonight, sitting over here?" Lester had a talent for remembering his customers' names, pretty much from the second time they came to the restaurant. This had always impressed Bick, a computer software sales rep who took great pride in his own ability to remember names.

"No. I just wanted to smoke."

"I didn't know you smoked. How's business?"

"Great," Bick answered gloomily.

Lester turned toward Melba as he poured the wine into a carafe. "And yours?"

"Better than I deserve," Melba said, lowering her head but keeping her eyes on Lester's. Melba was an interior designer. Her clients, the majority of whom were doctors, generally ignored her advice. They all seemed to want pictures of sunlit meadows or moonlit seashores in chrome frames. Melba had long ago learned to laugh off what her clients did or did not do with her decorating advice, so long as they paid her fees.

Bick was less cavalier about his work. He despised being a salesman and took every lost sale personally.

"You look nervous tonight," Lester said, patting Bick's shoulder as he left their booth.

You got that right, Bick thought. A moment passed. He studied the knobiness of his knuckles.

"Well. Here we are in the smoking section," Melba sighed.

"Yeah . . ."

"I never thought I'd see *you* here. It puts you in a whole new light."

He'd had his last cigarette two hours ago. He'd thought only minutes before they walked in the restaurant that he really wanted one, but now he felt as if his intention to be totally honest tonight was adolescent, self-indulgent. To the best that he could tell so far, it made no difference to Melba whether he smoked or not.

He watched her pour herself a full glass of wine and nearly drain it.

"Ummm," she said, her eyes closed then suddenly open and boring into him with their smile. "Let's get drunk tonight. We haven't done that in *ages*."

True, thought Bick. If by *ages* you mean one week.

Glancing up at the poster of a wine bottle on the wall beside their booth, Melba felt vaguely romantic. One of her clients, a lean, blond, scuba-diving dentist whom she'd guessed to be five or six years younger than she, had made a pass at her late that afternoon. He'd told her she seemed girlish. And what, exactly, was that supposed to mean, she'd asked him. He said she probably hadn't done half the things in bed that she'd thought of, and that she hadn't thought of half the things that could be done.

She tried to appear unruffled. "Do you want the murals of Greek statuary or not."

"Barns. I grew up in the country. I hated every minute of it. I ended up in the city. I hate it here, too. I want pictures of barns. Old, red, collapsing ones."

"And do we want hay on the office floor?"

"Maybe."

"I happen to know a barn painter. He's a dentist. Just like you."

Now, as Melba looked around and studied the posters at Romeo's, she realized how perfectly the rain stains on the walls matched the stains on the posters. Life could seem so simple and unified for entire moments at a time, she decided.

Melba drained her glass and poured another. She watched Bick, who seemed evasive and bleak. "Well?" she said.

"Well what?"

"Are you going to smoke?"

He'd been watching a young, noisy couple coming down the steps, and now he looked at Melba. "In a minute."

"Do you think I'm girlish?"

He shrugged. "Do I think you're girlish? No. You seem very settled and successful. To me, girlish means you'd be a bit on the silly side. Rash. Impulsive. But you told me you'd gotten over that."

"You don't think I'm rash and impulsive?"

"No."

"Not even in the good sense?"

"No." He reached in his suit jacket and brought out a maroon pack of Dunhill cigarettes. "Why, do you *want* to be rash and impulsive?"

She looked away, aware she was smiling. "I already am."

Bick studied her uneasily, not wanting to know what she might mean by such an admission.

Melba poured herself a third glass of wine. It was going down nicely, she thought, and her head was already light and free. "So, are you going to smoke or not?"

Bick took out a cigarette, looked at it, then set it in the ashtray. He began to feel stupid for the mood he was in. He told himself to keep talking.

"I lost my biggest client today."

She smiled. "Well, if it's any consolation, Dearest, I *got* my biggest. We won't lose a dime between us."

"Congratulations."

His tone made her look at him. "You seem a little too enthusiastic. Should I run and hide before you hit me?"

That made him laugh. He loosened his tie, unbuttoned his neck, and picked up the cigarette. He lit it, puffed it, smiled at her.

"This is too much," she said, shaking her head as the smoke escaped toward her. She told herself to go along with it, let him get relaxed for the announcement she was about to deliver.

"So," she said. "Tell me something else I don't know about you."

Bick tried to hold his grin and not appear alarmed by how accurately she'd read his intentions. His heart began to trip painfully and his vision blurred. He struggled to speak.

"I think we should get divorced."

MELBA STARED, stunned that he had usurped her own announcement. She decided not to tell him that she totally agreed, lest she weaken her bargaining position.

"Divorced," she said, without inflection.

Bick nodded gravely. "Yeah."

She smiled. "Just out of curiosity, why?"

He shrugged. His eyes were red. "Don't you think we've lost the passion in our—"

"You can't lose what you've never had."

His eyes traveled to the cigarette in his hand. "Yeah, you're probably right about that."

A silence gathered as Melba tried quickly to inventory her feelings. She had always imagined that she, not Bick, would be the one who ended their relationship, if it ever needed to be ended. Bick looked pathetic, and she'd never been able to stomach a pathetic man, no matter how legitimate his reason for looking so.

Lester arrived at the table with an antipasto plate. "You folks are awfully quiet. How's that cigarette?"

Bick and Melba glared at him.

"Sorry," Lester said, backing away.

"Don't just leave," Melba said. "At least bring us another bottle of wine."

Lester's departure brought back the silence. Melba watched Bick as Bick avoided her eyes.

"You don't seem terribly upset," he said to the table.

She shrugged with her mouth. "I'm trying to decide." She realized that her emotional inventory was becoming more complex. She had grown fond of Bick in simple, comfortable ways that made her smile to pick up his socks or put his back scratcher in the drawer where it belonged, or water his three house plants when he was away. He had always let her pick out his clothes at the store and then decide for him each morning what he would wear. If nothing else, Bick was easy to live with. There had never been a struggle for control of the household; Melba had seized it the day they moved in together, and Bick had never protested. And although her feelings toward him did lack passion, she had never thought she needed much passion in her life. At least, not until she met Lawrence the country dentist that afternoon.

"SHOULD I DECANT this or just pour it?" Lester asked. He seemed to sense the tension, and his smile was gone.

Melba nudged her glass an inch closer to the edge of the table. "Just pour."

As Lester poured, Bick drained his glass and set it down to be refilled. "Bring me a double Scotch the next time you come back." Bick stubbed out his cigarette and lit another.

Melba laughed as she turned to scan the room.

She was trying to be brave, Bick thought. Typical Melba and her fake toughness, trying to make light of something that was breaking her heart.

"I assume you have a *friendly* divorce in mind."

"Well, yes," Bick said.

"Forget it. I don't believe in friendly divorces. We don't have any children, so we have no excuse for pretending to be civil when we actually loathe each other."

"Do you loathe me?" he asked, watching her face change from a grimace to a smile to almost a sob to a sneer.

"Utterly," she said.

"Starting just now? Tonight?"

Lester came back with the Scotch. Melba waited until he was gone before she answered.

"Yes. Starting tonight."

"Good."

"Good?" Her voice rose. "Good?" Her voice rose higher yet, and heads began to turn. "You say *good?* Are you such an imbecile that you think my loathing you is *good?*"

Bick knew that trying to calm her down at this point would only make her angrier. "I only ask," he said quietly, "because I've often had a feeling that you've been loathing me for several years. If you just started tonight, maybe there's hope for us after all." Bick took a slug from the glass of Scotch. He felt his brain cool even as his throat warmed, finding relief in her scorn.

Sensing that the power was back in her lap, Melba let her smile grow in a slow, sinewy stretch until her cheeks ached. Her voice ran out of her like a fire engine.

"You are a perfect horse's ass! Haven't you even been inventive enough to look in my dresser drawer and see my *appliance*? It's right on top. I don't try to *hide* it."

"I don't rummage ..."

"Why do I need you?"

Bick felt his own voice rise. "For nothing. Obviously. I assume the damned thing can *cook*, too!"

"Better than you!"

"That's hardly a surprise."

"In fact, Gustav is everything I ever wanted in a man."

"Gustav? You're kidding, I hope."

"You're right. I am. Some days he's Serge. Or Pierre. Isn't that great? A regular United Nations."

The heads in the restaurant turned again, but Bick didn't care. It was all out on the table now. She'd get the house, he'd get the payment. He assumed she'd want the Caddy and he'd settle for the Ford. But that was okay; the divorce was almost over, and it was a good idea after all. But for now, he told himself, try to be nice.

"Look, I'm sorry . . ."

"Sorry?" Her voice rose in a grating whisper.

"Sorry I'm hurting you."

She laughed. "You flatter yourself."

"Then I'm sorry for that, too." Bick noticed that none of the customers was watching them anymore. Just Lester, who approached the table on tiptoes. He looked from Bick to Melba and back to Bick. "I don't suppose you're ready to order yet, are you?"

"God, yes," Melba said. "I'm famished."

THEY ORDERED simply, linguine and clam sauce for her, spaghetti with sausages and peppers for him. Lester was about to leave when Melba grabbed his sleeve. "Wait. We want your opinion on something."

Lester's smile turned nervous. "What took you so long?"

Bick squirmed. "Jesus, Melba . . ."

"Do you think Bick and I should get divorced?"

Lester looked slowly from one to the other. Melba got the impression he was trying to decide whether or not they were serious.

"Well, yes and no."

Melba snorted as she released his sleeve. "You can go back to the kitchen now, Lester. We'll call you if we need any more insight. In the meantime, please bring us another bottle of wine."

In the three minutes before Lester brought the salads, neither spoke but both of them smoked a cigarette. It was Melba's first since high school, and she merely held it. Smoking, she recalled, was at least as much a hand thing as a mouth thing. It was a look, not just an addiction.

Lester approached the table with the new bottle of wine. His deference struck Bick as very professional. Lester knew how to act around conflict; don't ignore it, but don't get involved, either.

"Well?" Melba asked. "Have you had time to decide our fate yet?"

"I'm not in the fate business," Lester said, his smile forced but not brittle.

"We're all in the fate business," Melba said. "It's just that some of us—you, for instance—insist on thinking it's only a hobby." She laughed at her joke and slapped lightly at the edge of the table.

"THE PROSPECT of divorce stimulates the appetite, don't you think?" Melba ate with a flourish. When she was drunk, any crisis could wait until after dinner. The salad and the pasta were more than food, she thought. They were an event. Everything about the evening was an event. It was the most exciting night in the history of their relationship. That dentist who wanted the barn pictures was right; she had indeed not even scratched the surface of sexual possibility. She'd do him the first night she was unmarried. With any luck and efficiency, that could be tomorrow. Maybe she'd do him in the afternoon, right in his office, on that hay she was planning to have scattered on his floor.

Bick felt a new surge of drunken resolve, convinced that he was on the verge of ironing out his entire life.

"I don't mean to embarrass you, but—"

"I wasn't even close to being embarrassed. But thanks for your consideration."

Bick ignored her. "But . . . your . . . appliance, it's *smaller* than me. Isn't it?"

"Ha! So you *do* rummage."

"Yes. Once. I'm sorry. But, it is smaller—"

Her jaws stopped working as she stared at him. "So?"

"Well, I'll admit, it didn't make me feel insecure. The way something like that can make any man feel kind of inadequate." Bick sat back, and, trembling, lit another cigarette. His gaze wandered toward the kitchen, where Lester stood leaning against the door frame. The one glance prompted Lester to the table again.

"So, are we finished?"

Melba and Bick glanced at each other for the first time in several minutes and nodded.

Lester picked up their plates. "One thing I hate about divorce is it always means I lose customers. Coming here reminds one of them of the other, so they both stay away."

"Oh. Well, hell, that's a good reason for us to stay together," Melba said. "Don't want to be bad for business."

"The thing is," Lester went on, looking easily from one to the other, "the thing is that I really like you people. You're good folks. You fight all the time, but so what?"

Bick and Melba looked at each other. The smile broke first on Melba's face, then spread across the booth to Bick's.

"We only fight here," Melba said.

Bick slugged down the last of his Scotch, but Melba continued to sip gently from her glass of wine as Lester headed back to the kitchen with their plates.

Hours later, after Lester had left them a key and gone home, Bick and Melba still sat talking. They were too drunk even to hold their heads up, and eventually they slept, heads on the table, holding hands.

Some Kind of Brave

WHEN LORETTA TOLD Morton she wanted to use her five-thousand-dollar inheritance to open a hotdog stand down by the lake, he was instantly opposed and pointed out all kinds of ways they could use the money better. They could build an extension on their small grocery store in town and sell hotdogs there, if she was so bent on selling hotdogs. They could put a new roof on the house. They could buy a better car and not look quite so poor to everyone else in town. They could buy some *new* clothes for a change rather than having to drive to the thrift store in Gadsden to pick through the secondhand racks.

"A hawdawg stand?" His puffy eyes and fat lips scrunched up with scorn. "A damned *hawdawg* stand. Where they ain't nobody but six months out of the year. And prob'ly don't none of 'em eat hawdawgs."

But she held firm and said it was something she'd always wanted to try, having her own business.

"When did you get the idea you wanted your own business?" Mort demanded. "That's a new one on me."

"What difference does it make if I got the notion ten minutes ago? I just do."

Mort never looked her in the eye for long when they disagreed on things. His gaze would fall to her hefty middle and heftier hips, as if her arguments would be more valid if she were forty pounds slimmer and twenty years younger.

"I need you working at the store in town," he said.

"We got six kids, for God's sake," she countered. "You got all the help you need for the store. Me and Ned will run the hotdog stand."

Ned was their youngest, only five. He was a late baby, eight years younger than the next youngest, and Loretta had at first dreaded the idea of having to be a servant to yet another set of desires and demands. But Ned seemed different from the rest, more aware of his mother and her feelings. It was not having to mother Ned in her middle age that now bothered Loretta; it was having to mother the others, including Morton.

"Place is too far off the beaten track, Etta. Delivery truck ain't gonna want to drive all the way down to the lake."

"Then I'll carry what I need out yonder myself."

"It'll cost more'n five thousand to open up."

"I called a secondhand place in Cullman. They got a cooler, a steam table, and a sandwich bar for six hundred. Sydney Carter says he can build a place for two thousand, with wiring and plumbing."

Morton shook his worried head. "They's all kinds of *nuts* around here in the summertime. You could get robbed and killed."

"There's cabins and people all over the place down on the lake road," she said. "I ain't gonna get robbed and *killed.*"

Morton's fleshy jowls quivered. His face was scarlet. "I said *no.* I ain't gonna let you waste good money like that." Mort slapped the table and glared at her. All six kids watched, their forks stopped on their plates, their jaws suddenly idle. Even the spring rain outside seemed to come to a momentary halt.

Loretta had figured it would be like this, Morton ordering her not to open her hotdog stand. She'd just stop mentioning it, she told herself. Let him figure he'd won, and then one morning she'd put Ned in her old DeSoto and drive to her hotdog stand for opening day. Morton and the boys would have to make their own breakfast, do the wash, feed the chickens, run the grocery store, and generally take care of themselves.

The big morning arrived two months after she'd first told Morton what she was planning to do. She'd made no mention of it since then, until the night before she planned to open.

"What's all them Co-Colas and tater chips doing in your trunk?" he asked her at supper.

"I'm opening up tomorrow."

"Opening up *what?*"

"My hotdog stand."

Morton's face stiffened, his graying, crew-cut hair seemed to stand a little taller, and the chunk of meatloaf he held on his fork an inch in front of his mouth tumbled down the bib of his overalls onto his lap. For once his eyes did not leave hers, and it was Loretta who finally looked away.

"I'm a sum bitch," he said quietly. He dropped his fork on his plate, backed away from the table with a slow scrape of his chair, and stared at her. "I'm a sum bitch."

LAKE ROAD was semi-deserted from October until April, except for the hunters and a few of the older folks who still came to fish instead of going up nearer to Guntersville. In the summertime, though, Lake Road was different, coming to life with a few dozen families who had cabins there, in spite of the pocked road that often got washed away each spring when the creeks flooded. The people who owned the camps just had more crushed limestone hauled in, and then their car tires and feet crunched along, audible from half a mile away, until the stone settled and the summer rains packed it down.

Along with her five thousand in cash, Loretta had also inherited an acre of land there on Lake Road, and this was where she had her hotdog stand put up, after a spot was cleared and the pine and oak logs hauled off to the lumberyard. It was a small cinderblock box, more of a shed than a cabin, with a roof that slanted from front to back. Loretta painted the outside walls to make them look, from a distance at least, like logs. Beside the shack, under the high shade of the old pines, were four picnic tables where her customers could sit down to eat her slaw dogs, her chili dogs, and her own special-sauce Etta Dogs, which were loaded with browned onions. The soft drink cooler was the old-fashioned kind with the lift-up lid, filled with ice chunks that Loretta chipped with an ice pick from the big blocks that the Pepsi Cola truck brought her. The capped necks of the Pepsi and Buffalo Rock bottles seemed to grow out of the ice itself.

Once the aroma of hotdogs and French fries began to saunter down Lake Road, Loretta got the dribble of business she'd hoped for—nine hotdogs the first day, nineteen the second, twenty or more every day thereafter. By the end of July, she was taking in about fifty dollars a day, twenty- five after expenses.

Each afternoon, Etta watched the husbands drive out from their offices in town to their cabins on the lake to join their wives and children, and for once she felt no resentment that the women driving these clean, undented cars did not have to work, as she always had. She did not feel inferior to them or their expensive bathing suits and tennis shorts and sandals as they trooped up Lake Road to buy her hotdogs—not the way she used to feel when she saw them in town. Nor did she find their children snooty; she knew they were actually much better behaved than her own. There was a polite envy in the scrubbed children's eyes, Loretta saw, for Ned, who had domain over that cooler full of chunked ice and soda bottles. None of them had invited Ned to come to their camps to swim with them, but Loretta sensed that such a possibility was not out of the question. One day. Maybe.

She did not wish to be someone else, as she used to. She did not look in the mirror and see only her age, her fat. Instead, she took great pride in counting the money in her cash register—two or three times a day, when she wasn't busy serving hotdogs. She took a childish pleasure in telling herself she would not turn any of it over to Morton; she'd already made plans to invest her profits in an ice cream freezer next month.

"What're you doing with all that money," he asked her often.

"All what money?"

"I heard you was actually sellin' a few hawdawgs."

"You spying on me?"

"All's I know is we need a new beer cooler at the store. And I need a new chain saw and a new pickup. Let's shut that damn fool hawdawg stand down and put what money you got left to some *decent* use."

Her hotdog business *was* a decent use, she told herself. She worked hard from ten in the morning until just after one. During the slow afternoons, Loretta read romance magazines and relaxed, sometimes napping, her head on her arms as she sat at one of her picnic tables. The only sounds came from the drone of an occasional plane, or the muffled screeches of children as they splashed around down at the lake. Loretta's favorite sound was the light afternoon breeze as it rustled against the screen door and made the springs creak faintly. When Morton offered to oil the hinges, she told him to leave the door just like it was. She could see it made him half crazy that she didn't need his help.

In August, Morton *forgot* to pay the light bill, which cost her a day's business before the electricity got turned back on. After that, she paid the light bill herself. Then Morton forgot to order her supplies, including hotdogs and buns, from the Gadsden delivery truck that stopped at their store twice a week. Loretta drove down to Gadsden and found a different supplier, one with fatter, pinker hotdogs, who was willing to make the drive all the way to Lake Road—and give her a better price than the supplier Morton knew.

Ned spent the days stripped down to his bathing suit and smeared with war paint as he played in the field and woods behind the hotdog stand. Loretta had a cow bell that she rang every hour or so. Ned didn't have to come in when she rang it, only make an appearance. Sometimes, when it was rainy or Ned was just plain tuckered out from stalking all the imagined warriors from rival tribes, he napped in a big cardboard carton full of rags that Loretta had fixed for him next to the drink cooler.

That was where he was the night of the robbery.

NED HAD JUST awakened and looked outside at the falling dark when the two men came into the store. They didn't seem to notice him right away. The first one wore an army jacket and had a Halloween vampire mask over his face. His belly strained at the snaps on his jacket as if two invisible claws were trying to pull the jacket apart. Ned thought Army Jacket must have been hot, wearing all those clothes and breathing so loud. The other man, very tall, very thin, wore a baseball cap, and his face was blackened with what looked like old engine grease. He nudged the door shut with a shotgun.

"Shut out all the lights," Army Jacket hollered.

Loretta's trembling arm reached behind her and slapped at the wall, trying to find the light switch without looking. When she spun her head to see where to direct her flailing hand, her glasses flew off onto the floor.

"Just leave 'em," Army Jacket ordered. "Hit them lights."

As her fumbling hand found the lightswitch and brushed it, the store fell to darkness. Army Jacket turned on a big flashlight, the kind that's a box with a big eye on the front. In the darkness, the beam from the flashlight shook about the store, then came back to the cash register.

"Lay down on that there floor, lady. On your stomach with your hands behind your head. Get that kid over here, too." The beam shot directly into Ned's eyes, and he put his hand up in front of his face.

"Get down there beside her!"

Ned did as he was told. In the dark his foot came down on his mother's glasses. Ned heard her cry out, as if he'd stepped on her finger.

Loretta yanked his sleeve and pulled Ned to the floor. The beam of the flashlight roamed around them. The cash register clanged. The drawer shot open. Hands rustled, flipping up the bill holders.

"Where's the rest at?" Army Jacket demanded.

"There ain't no more," Loretta said in quivers.

The voice became more vicious. "Don't you tell me that. Now where's the rest at?"

"He done picked it up already," she said between sobs. "He done took it away to the bank already."

"Lady, I'll blow your teeth out the backside your haid if you don't tell me where the damn cash is at."

Ned listened to her wheeze. "Ain't . . . none . . . I swear."

"They ain't twenty bucks there," Baseball Cap said, his voice calmer than Army Jacket's. "They's prob'ly a safe somewheres."

"Nobody said nothin' about no safe."

Things fell to the floor in soft thuds.

"They ain't nothing' but buns," Army Jacket said. "And hawdawgs."

The footsteps came back. The two men stood directly over Loretta and Ned, the pool of light glowering about them.

"I'm gonna' blow that little shit's brains out if you don't tell me where the damn money's at."

"No!" Loretta's arm shot out to cover Ned's head.

"Then tell me, goddam it."

Ned suddenly felt something warm and wet beginning to spread underneath him. He struggled to get up.

"Get back down, you—"

"But she done peed."

"Shuddup and git back down!"

Ned settled back onto the floor. Loretta grasped his shirt to hold him there. The end of the shotgun barrel came back into view, hovering before Ned's eyes. No one moved or said anything for a few moments, then the light moved away, once again sweeping over the walls and floor of the cabin. The voices dropped to a whisper. "They's a safe in here somewhere. I just *know* it."

"He didn't say nothin' about no . . ."

Ned stood up, and Loretta's hand closed around his ankle. "Get back down here," she whispered. But he continued to stand. She didn't argue. The robbers no longer struck her as dangerous, just stupid and mean.

"Let's just take that twenty in the register and scram," Army Jacket said. He turned around and shot the flashlight beam at Ned, and his voice rose to a frantic scream. "Why ain't you *on that floor?*"

"Cause it's wet down there."

Baseball cap and his gun came in back of the counter again. The end of the barrel settled against Loretta's head.

"One last time. Where's the rest of the money at?"

She played to them. "Oh, God save me. God save me."

The barrel of the gun crawled down her spine, making the flab on her arms twitch each time the barrel scraped another inch toward the bulge of her butt.

"I know there's money in here somewheres. I can feel it just like the way my knees ache when cold weather's coming."

"C'mon, damn it." Baseball cap moved a step toward the door.

Then Army Jacket said, "You stay down on that floor for ten minutes. Hear me? Or I'll come back and shoot the *both* of you." Loretta still held onto Ned's ankle as the screen door slammed. A car engine started. Ned jerked himself loose and ran to the door.

"Ned, come *here* and do what he said," Loretta's quivering voice ordered. They'll come back and shoot us." Loretta waited until she could no longer hear the car, then she struggled to her feet, her knees shaking wildly, and fumbled at the wall until she found the light switch. She looked at the floor, looked at her dress. She was soaked down the front. She looked at the crushed remnants of her glasses. She sat down heavily on an unopened carton of canned soft drinks and held her face in her hands. She thought she might cry, but she wouldn't let herself. Not in front of Ned. But when she took her hands away from her face and looked once more at the soaked front of her dress, it was her anger, not her fear, not her fatigue, that finally forced the quiet tears into her eyes.

WHEN MORTON'S pickup pulled up in front, about ten minutes later, Ned ran outside. "Daddy, Daddy, we was *robbed!*"

Morton came into the cabin and slowly looked around. Ned followed close behind.

"They almost *shot* us, Daddy."

Morton stood just behind the counter looking from the cash register to Loretta and back. "You two all right?"

Loretta neither answered nor looked at him.

He looked back at the cash register. "They get it all?"

She nodded slowly. "Yep. Every dime."

"How much?"

"About two thousand. Maybe three, I ain't counted it in a few days."

Morton whistled. "Two thou . . . but I thought you said you didn't have nothin' out here."

"Well, I guess I lied."

"Woman, I oughta smack you for keeping that kind of . . ." But Morton got hold of himself and just shook his head. "At least they didn't hurt you none."

She looked impassively at him. "How would *you* know?"

"Well, you look all right. And so does the boy. I guess we can be thankful for that. Say, what happened to your dress?"

"Momma had a accident," Ned said guiltily.

Loretta still held Morton in her iron eyes. "When people get scared, they have accidents."

Morton looked at her only a moment.

"Are we gonna go chase the robbers, Daddy?"

"No, son. Not tonight."

Morton seemed to cheer up quickly, Loretta thought, for a man whose household had just lost two or three thousand dollars. He smiled as he looked from her to Ned. "You done real good," he said to her. "Chase off two robbers." He turned toward Ned. "Get your Momma a Co-Cola. She's a brave one, ain't she?"

Ned even opened the bottle for her.

"Thank you," she said.

Ned's father shook his head. "Yes, sir. I believe both of you two was some kinda brave. You protected your momma, I bet, didn't you now?"

But Loretta felt Ned looking at her wet dress and the puddle on the floor. She knew that to him brave was something different from what she had done. To him, brave would have been shooting or hitting, not crying and shaking and wetting herself.

He shook his head. "Uh-uh. I wadn't brave."

His father hugged him roughly against his thigh for a moment, then gave him a little shove toward the drink cooler. "Sure you was. Get yourself a Co-Cola, too. An' git me one a them lemon ones. Let's close up and get on home. It's dangerous out here."

"Don't you think we oughta go to the police?" Loretta asked.

Morton cleared his throat. "I'll take care of it tomorrow. Let's just get home for right now."

"You'll take care of it like you took care of my light bill? And my potato chips and pickles?"

"I *said* I'll take care of it." They piled into the truck. Ned tried as best he could to stay away from the wetness on his mother's dress.

"Good," she said. She smiled inside as she imagined Morton and his cousins arguing and accusing each other over two thousand dollars the cousins could have found if they'd looked in her purse.

"I'm sure glad I have a man in my life to take care of things like that."

Thanh Ho Delivers

LATER, OF COURSE, Thanh would learn her way around the alleys of Southside as a cat learns its way through the tall grass of a vacant lot. The alleys and back streets were the fastest way to get where she was going, but for a long time after her first delivery, unlit places terrified her.

Thanh Ho Gourmet Pizza shop had opened exactly one year after Saigon was renamed Ho Chi Minh City. The only customers so far had been Mama's Vietnamese friends from church. They always came by to pick up their pizzas, commiserating for hours on end with Mama about how bad things must be back home and insisting that it was an imposition for Thanh's elder sister, Loc, to deliver the pizza to their homes. That's the point, Thanh tried to tell them; mine is the only pizza shop in the city of Birmingham that *delivers* pizza. But the Vietnamese people nodded and smiled and bowed and continued to pick up their pizzas. Only three orders, out of a total of fourteen, had been delivered.

Such a delivery service had been impossible until the family was reunited two weeks earlier, since Loc was the only member of the family who could drive or who had a car at her disposal. The three of them, Thanh, Loc, and Mama, scrubbed the shop inch by inch until the smell of Lysol reached half a block down the street. Even Mama, who grew up as a rich little princess in French Saigon, put on old clothes and got down on her hands and knees to scrub with the others. The shop was a rundown storefront in a neighborhood of peeling paint, potholed streets, and buckled sidewalks that were dangerous to walk on, let alone rollerskate on as the local children did. The shop itself consisted of a single large room with a small storeroom in which the Ho family spread its sleeping mats each night and watched Thanh's tiny TV with the sound turned down so as to have some light in the room and not just the unrelenting darkness to sleep in.

The bathroom was no larger than a closet; its fixtures were cramped— a tiny chin of a sink jutted over the toilet and its brown, wooden seat. The showerhead was mounted on a hose that hung meekly from the wall inside a circle of shower curtain. Thanh had not minded these living conditions during the month she had lived there by herself, exiled from the rest of the family when she had briefly dated a man of whom Mama disapproved. But when Loc and Mama joined her, Thanh saw that her shop was a humiliation, although Mama uttered no word of criticism. Mama had never failed to have an opinion about everything, but if she had one on Thanh's pizza shop, she kept it to herself.

Perhaps Mama really was wise—too wise to try to apply old opinions to new things of such momentous proportions as the family's future livelihood. Or perhaps she was simply not ready to shed the convenience and protection afforded by her status as reticent immigrant. Thanh was grateful for her mother's reserve. After being in America by herself for over a year, she would have had considerable difficulty taking orders again, at least in matters of basic money. Mama left the matter of making a living up to Thanh. She did, however, freely express her opinions on lesser matters: how Thanh and Loc should dress, and how they should conduct themselves in the presence of males, especially marriageable ones.

In spite of her attempts to observe and adjust to her new environment, Mama had brought many of the old ways from home. When Thanh told Mama how slow business was compared to what she had been accustomed to when she worked at Pizza Heaven, Mama burned some paper to change their luck. It was a custom among Vietnamese business people; you burned a piece of paper to chase away the incommodious spirit that had taken up residence in the shop and was crowding out the possibility of conducting commerce. The night's first order, from the Ngo family, came less than five minutes after Mama had tossed the ashes of the small paper bag into the toilet and flushed them away. Orders from the Ky and Giap families came soon after the Ngo family's pizza was in the oven and blossoming its aroma through the open door and into the spring evening street. A few orders came from Americans in the neighborhood who lived close enough to smell Thanh's oven.

The next night, orders came from over a mile away. Loc delivered them in the old Toyota that Gary Marsh, Loc's fiance, had lent them. The car had belonged to Gary when he was in college, and he'd never gotten around to selling it. The car had been in his garage for two years when Thanh noticed it and hinted to Gary that he should lend it to Elder Sister for making deliveries.

Within a very few days, the aromas of tomato and cheese, along with Gary's expensive colognes, fashioned the shop's tapestry of scents. Gary's family had sponsored Thanh—and later Mama and Loc—when Thanh Ho, twenty-five at the time but with the facial innocence of sixteen, first came to Birmingham from the placement center in Arkansas a year earlier. Gary, who was tall and gangly, struggling through his late twenties as the only unmarried member of his social set, treated Thanh with benign neglect while she was a guest in his home. But when Mama and Loc arrived three months ago, Gary immediately fell in love with Loc, who was beautiful by the standards of any culture, eastern or western. Loc was vivacious and yet restrained, an observer of humanity. It was from Elder Sister that Thanh had learned her own instinct to hear first and be heard second—and then only if others insisted on hearing what she might have to say.

Was Loc in love with Gary? Thanh was not sure. She often suspected that it was his money, not his character or personality, that had lured Elder Sister into such a hasty engagement. Gary's parents were clearly displeased with his selection of a mate, although they were unfailingly pleasant to Loc and her family. The discomfort of the Marshes was most apparent in the limitations that Gary now set upon Loc's behavior. She was not to take a job in a restaurant, not even as a hostess, although she'd been offered a job as a waitress at Mr. Ky's Asian Garden restaurant, where she could have made almost one hundred dollars a week. She was not to go anywhere alone, not even to the grocery store; Gary would drive her around to do whatever errands the family required.

And now Loc was delivering pizzas for Younger Sister. Thanh wondered with a mildly cruel delight what Gary and his pale, worried mother and flushed father thought about that, and how much of their dinner-table discussion had been devoted to the quaint little immigrant they had received from the seas who had started a business—with her own money.

Thanh guessed she was both a scandal for Gary's mother in terms of Loc's hold on Gary, and also a minor hero to Gary's father, who might have written operas about the romance of entrepreneurial adventure had he not been so busy expanding his already considerable ownings.

ABOUT A WEEK after the shop started to get regular calls for delivery, Thanh flunked her driver's license test. She had assumed she would pass the road test as easily as she'd passed the written exam when she applied for a learner's permit. So she insisted that Loc should, as planned, attend Gary's birthday party which was to be held that evening at the Mountain Brook Club. Thanh would handle the deliveries.

But as Thanh and Loc drove to the testing center, Thanh was aware of a pit in her stomach and the gnawing recognition of the many things she did not know how to make the car do. Backing up, for instance, still mystified her. How was one to back up without turning around, and how was one to turn around and still manipulate the steering wheel, brake, clutch? She'd tried only twice to back up, and both times she'd nearly hit something—a tree, a fence, other cars. But Gary had told many stories about people who were utterly incompetent as drivers and had licenses nonetheless—his mother, for instance. Thanh took heart from such stories. She knew beyond question that she had the potential to be an excellent driver, once she had the experience that having a license would allow her to gain.

Loc patted Thanh's thigh and got out. "Good luck."

As she pulled into the lanes where the examiners waited, Thanh thought the examiners looked stern and uncompromising, trained as they were to detect and enlarge human flaws. Thanh felt that she would need a compassionate examiner, and no such person was to be seen. When Thanh found herself next in line, the examiner who looked the least compassionate of them all approached the car. She was a thin, hard-faced black woman with wiry white hair and skeptical eyes that said she thought there were already too many drivers on the road.

Thanh looked away. The examiner walked around the car, looking at the tires. She ordered Thanh to turn on the head lights, the windshield wipers, the turn signals, and to blow the horn. She wanted to make sure the brake light worked. When the examiner opened the passenger door and got in, she glanced scornfully at the pillows under Thanh's legs and behind her back.

"You sure you're old enough to drive?"

"Yes," Thanh said. "I am twenty-six years old."

"If you say so. All right, go to the street, turn right and take the first left."

Thanh signalled, turned left, then signalled again and slid into the first opening in the traffic that allowed her to make the right turn. She felt that she had performed all the maneuvers perfectly.

"Turn around and go back to the testing center," said the examiner. "You didn't follow my directions."

Thanh's panic quickly gave way to the emptiness of defeat, and her tears fogged her eyes The examiner, who looked only straight ahead, pulled a tissue from her pocket and handed it to Thanh.

"It's dangerous to cry when you're driving," she said.

So, she is accustomed to such crying, Thanh thought bitterly. How cruel to carry tissues for people who cry when they fail the test!

"Find a place to turn around," the examiner said again. "There's a left turn lane up here. Make a u-turn, go back."

Thanh realized she was in the middle lane of a tight rush of traffic with no slot she could move into. She had unconsciously slowed down, and now the car behind her honked. She didn't dare turn her head to look for a spot in the left lane for fear that as she turned her head, she would pull the wheel in the direction of her eyes, as she was prone to do.

She finally remembered to use the turn signal, but as she watched the side-view mirror, she saw no one willing to let her into the lane. Her panic returned. Thanh felt as if she had been sucked into a vortex where only collision and death churned at the center.

The examiner rolled down her window and motioned above the car. A space opened up immediately. "Now!" she shouted.

Thanh wrenched the wheel too abruptly, and as they careened into the left lane, they sideswiped the guard rail. The car swerved wildly before the examiner grabbed the wheel. Thanh, paralyzed, had taken her foot off the accelerator.

"Drive this thing before you get us killed!"

Thanh's trembling foot tapped spastically on the gas pedal, causing the car to lurch. Her arms and shoulders had cramped in painful knots.

"Signal again. The turn lane's right up here."

Thanh coasted into the turn lane only to find herself once again unable to see a break in the oncoming traffic.

"Turn on your flashers. I'll drive us back."

They switched seats. The examiner calmed down the moment she was behind the wheel. "You're not quite ready to be driving in heavy traffic," she admonished gently. "Practice some more and come back in a few weeks."

All the way back to the testing center Thanh rode with her eyes on her lap, refusing to allow the tears out. In the car with Loc, Thanh was inconsolable, angry with herself and her life. Since leaving Saigon disguised as a boy on a dangerously small fishing boat, nothing had been easy. She hated to recall that life—playing dead to escape rape when Thai pirates boarded their boat and robbed everyone; trying to grab fish out of the sea as she floated for weeks with a dead man in the remains of the boat after it had broken up in a typhoon, then eating the fish raw and still alive the first time she actually mustered the courage to grab one; begging for food in the refugee camp in Malaysia, and selling a picture of herself naked to a camp doctor so that she would finally be allowed to pass the physical exam required for resettlement in the United States. Convincing herself to have sex with the fat old man who owned her shop so that he would not charge her rent for the first three months. And having to go to church with Mama every Sunday once the family was reunited, but not receiving communion and having to make excuses about why she didn't, unwilling as she was to go to confession since she no longer believed in the God who had failed to spare her from the Thai pirates who raped her, dead or not, once they figured out that she was not the boy she was dressed to be.

Nothing had been easy, and she knew it was likely that nothing ever again would be. Certainly not since the old days when the earthiest experience she'd ever had was to smell the freshly breast-fed baby of one of her friends in Saigon.

ONCE SHE HAD calmed down and accepted her failure to pass the driving exam, Thanh decided to make the deliveries that evening, license or no license, and urged Loc to attend Gary's party. They agreed to lie and told Mama that Thanh had passed. When Gary arrived to pick up Loc, he beamed a congratulatory smile. Thanh knew he was also congratulating himself for being the one who taught her to drive.

The pizza orders started coming in at five-thirty. Thanh showed Mama how to take an order over the phone, making a check mark on the order form that Thanh had designed, using numbers to indicate the configuration of ingredients that the customers would want. Although Mama had made great strides in learning English numbers, she clearly did not like the idea of being left alone while Thanh was out delivering.

"Just ask them what number, Mama. If they call, that means they have a copy of this order form. Make a mark in one of these boxes and get the phone number. I'll call them to get the address when I come back from delivering. I've written down the ingredients for each pizza in Vietnamese. You can get them in the oven so they'll be ready to deliver."

Thanh could see the fret on Mama's face. Her wrinkles grew so deep whenever she worried that no words were needed.

The first pizza went to a small house just two blocks from the shop. Thanh was only a little nervous as she drove, and she told herself that she would do just fine as the night progressed. When she returned, Mama said another order had come in, but she was unable to understand the phone number, so the order was lost. Thanh took the next order herself, and when the pizza was ready, she felt very good about driving as she carried the steaming box to the car. She was always a little uneasy pulling out of a parking space, but once the car was in motion, Thanh felt as if she'd been driving since she was born. She had already relegated the distant morning's disappointment to its proper status, and now her favorite thing about driving—that it was the key to her freedom—galloped back into her heart. The needs and aspirations of her family seemed almost manageable at such moments as these. She could imagine the method by which her shop would grow and prosper, and the small army of people she would one day need to hire to deliver her famous pizza all over the city, perhaps one day all over the country.

She recognized that these were not the thoughts of Ho Dinh Thanh of Saigon. In American she was Thanh Ho, a businesswoman. Ho Dinh Thanh had been only a student and a wisher for things she couldn't even name.

Thanh reminded herself to pay attention to the address she had written on the pizza box. She knew she was on the right street, but it was a section of the street with which she was not familiar. After two more blocks, the numbered avenue became a named street, and she decided she should retrace her path; she knew her way only on numbered streets and avenues. But one named thoroughfare led to another, and the streets became narrow and void of people, lined with small houses instead of apartment buildings.

Although she assumed she was not on the right street, she stopped when she saw a house number that corresponded to the one on the pizza box. The windows of the house were dark, but even from the street she thought she saw a flicker of light, a candle perhaps, creep around the edges of the drawn blinds. At the top of three brick steps, an arched portal framed the darkness, not quite revealing a door.

Thanh carried the pizza with her so that she could show the address on the box and ask directions.

In the dark portal she could not find a doorbell, so she knocked politely. No one came to the door, so she rapped harder. It opened slowly. Thanh readied a pleasant smile, but when the door stopped and no porch light came on, she held her breath. The pungent scent of something burning trickled from the darkness, making her eyes water.

A man's voice. "Yes?"

She forced herself to speak. "You order pizza?"

A pause. The voice seemed curious. "Pizza?"

"Yes. You order pizza?"

A light came on over Thanh's head. An unshaven man with long blond hair tied in a ponytail peered at her. He wore a dark bathrobe and no shoes.

"Nooo." His deep voice rose as he drew out the single syllable. "What do you mean when you say *order* a pizza?"

"You call. I make your pizza and deliver it."

The man smirked. "You don't say?"

Thanh could not help smiling. "Yes. I say."

"Well. I don't recall ordering a pizza. Then again, I can't say as I recall much of anything." A silly, staccato laugh rattled from him as he shoved the door all the way open and turned to address the others in the room behind him.

"Did anyone order a pizza?"

Two more people gathered at the door. At first Thanh was not sure if they were men or women. They both had long hair, but it was well groomed, stylized, and their clothes were not sloppy. A third person, whose reddish hair was permed, approached, his glazed eyes fixed on Thanh. She began to find all four of them unsettling with their probing, invasive smiles. They began to murmur among themselves, and Thanh decided that their voices were unquestionably male.

"Would you care to come in and join us?" the one in the robe asked. "It's time for the ancient hashish ritual. We could all get hungry and sacrifice a virgin or something. Ha ha. Is your pizza a virgin?"

"Or are *you?*" one of the others asked. That sent them into a fit of clucking sounds and head-back screeches as they careened about, bumping into each other in the doorway.

Thanh suspected that hashish was a drug. She became impatient.

"Maybe you tell me where I find this address?" She tilted the box for them to see.

"You don't like our party," the robed man said. "But we'll take that pizza, thank you." When he reached for the pizza, Thanh abruptly yanked it away.

"You know where I find address?"

"Right here," Lenny said. "And you intimated it was free."

"Not free. You want, you pay."

"She doesn't like us," the robed man repeated. "Let's send her away."

One of the others looked at him. "You mean . . . *the* way? Lenny, you said you weren't ever going to do that again."

Robed Lenny laughed. "I lied. As usual. I find this alien bumptious, bothersome, and, worst of all, stingy. I mean, I *want* that pizza."

Thanh understood little of their conversation and turned to leave.

"Wait," Lenny said. He stepped onto the porch and touched the metal address number on the wall beside the door. "I'll confess. This isn't the real number. We swapped with that house down there. The fourth one down."

Thanh became more confused. "What?"

"We swaped addresses to play a joke on the new postman. You should take the pizza down there."

The others groaned and went inside the house. "You're sick, Lenny," one of them said.

Lenny held out his arms to the side, and the sleeves of his robe seemed almost like wings. "Some girls swap clothes, others swap addresses. I'm sure they're waiting for their pizza. Fourth house."

"You're such a bitch, Lenny," one of the others said from inside.

Thanh fled as quickly as she could without openly running. The house to which Lenny had directed her was smaller and had no arch over the porch steps. Even in the dark, Thanh sensed that the place was more rundown, but at least here lights glared behind the plain white shades. She pushed the lighted doorbell button. The door cracked open immediately, but only enough to reveal an eye. Thanh forced herself to speak.

"You order pizza?"

"Say what?"

"You order pizza. I am deliver to you."

The door and the eye remained motionless for several seconds, but then Thanh felt the eye wander down the front of her body and stop. The door opened wide on two men, one in only bluejeans with a thin, hairy chest and shoulders, the other in soiled military fatigues. Their eyes sawed at her.

"Sure, sweetheart," the shirtless one said. "We ordered a pizza. Come on in." He had long black hair and a beard, and Thanh thought he would have been handsome had his eyes not been so full of smiling hatred. Although her heart clattered in her throat, Thanh tried to appear calm as she moved a step closer. The smell of a cat box drew her eyes to the far corner of the room. On the floor lay piles of clothes and scattered plastic forks, crumpled paper bags, cardboard food containers, newspapers, and dozens and dozens of dented beer cans whose sweetly stale odor was as strong as that from the cat box. The only piece of furniture in the room was a table, and an enormous gray cat lay among the dirty dishes suckling three kittens. Thanh's eyes watered, and she thought she might gag. Neither man made a move to take the pizza or pay her. She shrank into herself as she felt the one in the army uniform look her over.

"You Vietnamese, sweetheart?"

"Yes. I am."

"You boom-boom girl?"

Thanh's indignation instantly overwhelmed both her fear and her revulsion. "No! You pay me now, I leave!"

"Pay you?" They smirked at each other again. "We was war heroes in your piss-ant country, sweetheart. I think you owe us a pizza at the very goddam least. Maybe even a little thank-you blowjob."

Thanh knew she should turn and run but she was too slow. The shirtless man's arm shot out and grasped her shirt, but she stomped with all of her one hundred pounds on his bare foot, turning up her foot to make sure it was her heel that landed. His hand flew free, and she ran up the street to her car, the man's curses following her. She threw the pizza into the backseat as she jumped in and locked all the doors. In a moment of perfect chance, her trembling fingers managed the key directly into the ignition. The tires squealed when she popped the clutch too fast, and she swerved toward cars parked along the street, all of them a blur. She yanked the wheel back and forth, trying to regain control without slowing down. She pictured the men in their own car, chasing her, getting closer, leaping over her car and blocking her.

Her galloping heart crowded her breathing, but she kept driving. When she finally allowed herself to cry, her rage had displaced her fear. If only the license examiner had let her drive at night, filled with terror for her life, and fleeing between the tight rows of parked cars, Thanh thought.

SHE CAME TO a busy avenue and turned right, since that was much easier than trying to turn left. In the distance to her right she saw the downtown skyline, which meant she was heading away from the university neighborhood rather than back toward it. She reached behind her to feel the pizza box and found it no longer tepid, let alone hot. As was the case that morning, the heavy traffic had her trapped in a middle lane and she could not find a way to make a turn that would bring her back toward her shop. Only once before had she driven at night, and now she was blinded by the rush of headlights that swarmed around her. When she finally sensed a break in the traffic that would allow her to change lanes and get off the busy street, she turned onto a small, dark street with deep, jolting potholes and depressing apartment buildings where people sat on steps and stared as she ambled by. The beams of her headlights quivered over the crumbled pavement as she aimlessly roamed along each new street and lowered herself deeper into the pit of night.

Thanh stopped at the first brightly lighted convenience store she came to and waited in her locked car near the door until someone who didn't terrify her came out. It was a young black woman. Thanh rolled down her window and asked the woman how to get to the university.

"I'm heading that way. You just follow me."

"You very kind," Thanh said. "You like a pizza? Cold now, but just put in oven and warm again." She opened the box and held it out the window.

The woman's nostrils flared with interest, but then she began to scowl. "Shrimp? On a pizza? And pineapple?"

"Is so delicious. Dried tomatoes and feta cheese, too."

The black woman cautiously took the box from Thanh. "My old man will eat anything," she said. "You follow me; I'll show you how to get back to Southside."

She drove so fast it scared Thanh to try to keep up with her. A few blocks from her shop, Thanh began to recognize streets. Her relief was mixed with admiration for Elder Sister as Thanh tried to imagine what kinds of ordeals Loc must have encountered on her deliveries. It was typical of Loc that she had never once complained. When Thanh finally pulled up in front of the shop, Mama was at the door.

"Where have you been, child?"

Thanh knew she couldn't tell her mother what she'd just been through, so she merely shrugged. "I got lost."

"The phone rings constantly, and I can't understand a single word anyone says. They just hang up on me."

Thanh felt her calm as almost a force within her, so glad was she to be back home. "I know, Mama," she said.

Gary and Loc pulled up in front of the shop and sat in the car talking for several minutes before they came in. Loc seemed subdued, and Thanh wondered if Elder Sister and Gary had quarreled. Mama openly stared as the two sat down at the table, neither speaking nor looking at each other.

"Well," Loc finally said. "Shall we play cards?"

Thanh touched Loc's shoulder as she walked by her. "I had no idea what you were going through out there."

Loc looked puzzled. "What do you mean?"

"How strange these Americans are. So dangerous."

Loc shrugged with the down-turned corners of her mouth. "I don't know what you're talking about."

Gary stared from one sister to the other. "Translation, please. You wouldn't want me to feel left out, would you?"

When Thanh looked at Gary she felt sad for him. If only he didn't look like such a jerk, she thought, and didn't have such a careful family that looked at everyone they saw with so many ways to judge them. If only each of them, Gary, his mother, Mr. Marsh could spend one night delivering pizza, perhaps Gary would finally become worthy of Elder Sister.

"Too complicate," Thanh said. "Impossible translate. Happy birthday. Why you home so early from party? Boring?"

Gary laughed. "Kind of. I didn't want to admit it, but I believe you're right."

Mama mumbled something, then jumped when the phone rang again. Thanh picked up the receiver and answered in the sweetest voice she could muster.

"Hello, this a Thanh Ho Gourmet Pizza. How many pizza you order tonight?"

Straight to Belize

BILLY'S, OR BELIZE, as Wyatt and Jay called the place, was a light green cinder block beer joint that had been built as a filling station. It was a neighborhood bar, but not for the neighborhood in which it was located. Billy had moved his business from a white neighborhood when the rent got too high, and his customers followed along, the way a congregation might follow its pastor to a new church. Now Billy's was on the last shabby fringe of an upscale restaurant district. His customers were white, working class folks, mostly men and most of them middle-aged. The neighbors were poor blacks, who had been given to understand from Day One that they were not welcome in the bar. Billy's customers came and went without noticing the home folks, and the residents ignored Billy and his customers as if the bar were nothing more than a shoddy mural painted on a fence on that corner. Conflict was avoided because contact was avoided.

Wyatt and Jay went there for the cheap, under-used pool tables—twenty-five cents a game, usually no wait. They began to call the place Belize after concluding that it was a third-world bar. The inside walls were lined with cardboard cases of empty beer bottles and parts of some car engine or air-conditioning unit that Billy was working on. It was dark and hot in the bar in spite of the cool looking neon beer signs and a large ceiling fan that worked up a stiff breeze. But the fan just spun the hot air around, and Billy refused to turn on the AC unless the temperature inside reached at least ninety-five.

It was even hotter in the pool room, and Billy refused to turn on the AC in there at all. He claimed it was broken. But if all three pool tables were in use, the AC suddenly fixed itself. Wyatt had noticed how Billy turned it on, so Wyatt always turned it on himself. Billy, who was squat, bald, bearded and about forty, would appear in the doorway between the two rooms and look surprised.

"Oh, that thing finally come on?"

"It's magic, Billy," Wyatt would say. "I can walk into any place in town, and all the AC units burst into action."

A thin, blue layer of smoke from the previous night hovered in the light above the pool table, and Wyatt swatted at it with his cue stick while Jay labored to get the triangle of balls tight.

"I hate this place," Wyatt said. "Why do we come here?" Wyatt was tall and lean and wore executive glasses and a thin, neat mustache. He was too well groomed to fit in at a place like Belize. The regulars ignored the few suits who wandered into the place, usually by accident. But Jay and Wyatt had been coming to Belize for about three years and had gained a curious acceptance.

Jay, whose real name was Dexter, worked as a graphic designer at an ad agency. He wore his hair shoulder-length and his curly, clipped beard made his face look chubby and almost kind. Jay never wore suits and refused to attend events at which a suit and tie were the expected attire.

"Because you're a celebrity here," Jay said.

Wyatt happened to look a lot like Carter Standish, the last white man who had run for mayor against the three-term black incumbent.

"Mr. Standish," the guys around the bar would ask when they saw Wyatt, "do you think we'll beat that black bastard this time?"

"I don't know," Wyatt always said. "I believe it all depends on how much you people donate to my campaign fund. A Diet Sprite might make me feel I had a fighting chance."

Everyone at the bar, even stoic Billy, always laughed, even though the exchange never varied.

"You're a good man," Nick the Grik always said, gripping Wyatt's biceps so tightly that the tendons in back of the old man's bony fingers stood out like welts. Nick's neat white hair was brushed straight back. He'd taken to wearing a suit to the bar every night, now that he was trying to court Jamie Salver, who, at fifty, was thirty years younger than Nick.

When Wyatt went to the bar to order a Diet Sprite for himself and a beer for Jay, he noticed that Nick the Grik was not there, even though Jamie Salver sat at the bar talking with Big Faye.

"Where's the old man tonight?"

Billy shrugged. "He ain't been around for a couple of days. I ain't sure where he's at." Billy leaned a little closer and lowered his voice. "His operation didn't work out like he planned."

"Operation?"

"You ain't heard about that? He was having one of them inflatable peckers put in, but it didn't work. He figured that was why Jamie didn't want to marry him." Billy smiled. "Ain't that the damdest thing you ever heard?"

"Kind of."

"You're a lawyer. You ought to help him sue that goddam hospital. It cost him every fuckin' dime he had to his name. Life savings."

"THAT WAS JUST what I needed to hear the night before I have outpatient surgery," Wyatt said when he returned to the pool room with the drinks and told Jay the story.

Jay smiled. "I hate that it didn't work, but you have to admire the old guy for trying, huh?"

"If you were old and in love with a much younger woman, would you do it?"

Jay shook his head no. "I doubt if I'll have to worry about getting old. Break 'em up."

The break was weak, Jay noticed. The hard little lump under Wyatt's collarbone had been growing for the past two months and was now the size of a grape. The balls tumbled around the table but nothing fell.

Wyatt held up a finger. "See? I got a paper cut at work today. Those things are painful."

Jay did a chicken cluck as he lined up a shot. "Bwak, bwak, bwak." He ran in six balls before he missed.

"You *are* going to let me win tonight, aren't you?"

"Of course," Jay said. "Shoot."

Wyatt ran in three balls and missed, leaving Jay an easy shot on his last ball and an even easier shot on the eight. Wyatt gave him a hard look.

"I'll build a big lead and let you come storming back," Jay said. "You like it best that way, don't you?"

They had known each other for nearly ten years and had long ago agreed that their friendship proved that opposites do attract. Jay was an aging hippie; Wyatt had been a fighter pilot in Vietnam. The pool table was their forum for discussion of all things, ranging from what was wrong with the human race to what was wrong with Wyatt that made him feel so unrelentingly lonely and insecure.

"It's the hairdo," Jay told him. "You're just too neat. You could grow a tremendous afro if you weren't so anal. And do criminal law instead of that boring corporate stuff."

They had agreed that there was nothing wrong with Jay; he was simply psychotic. Once that fact was established, his every thought, action and utterance could be seen as totally consistent with every other. The secret to life, according to Jay, was to take grave matters lightly, ignore the merely important, and pretend to take the insignificant seriously, so as to fit in with others.

Wyatt was unable to share this view, driven as he was by a strangling sense of guilt. There was no explaining it; he was not Catholic, Jewish, or Southern Baptist. But he flew to Dallas every month to visit his mother— and grew morbid if he missed a month. Wyatt was at his grimmest in the early stages of any relationship in which he hoped to sleep with the woman he was seeing. After the first bedding, however, his guilt turned to anxiety as he groped for ways to end each inevitably imperfect relationship.

"So, how's Sylvia?" Jay asked as Wyatt racked.

"She's driving me nuts. I made the mistake of telling her that I keep a diary. She asked me if I'd written about her. When I said yes, she said she had a right to see it."

"She's a big girl. You think she can't handle the truth about how you feel toward her?"

"Correct."

Jay lined up his break, nosing his stick toward the cue ball in long, slow strokes. "I once got rid of a girlfriend that way. I didn't even really keep a journal, but I got one just for her. I wrote some bad stuff in it, left it on the table while I went out to the store for more beer. When I came back, she was gone." Jay rammed the white ball into the others with an ear-rattling crash. The balls raced around the table. Three of them fell.

"That was pretty low, Jay."

"Yeah. I know."

Jay shot in five stripes, then made a two-cushion shot on the corner pocket. He gasped as the cue ball almost followed the eight down the hole, stopping a hair short. Next game, Jay sank the eight ball on the break.

"Are you sure you're planning to let me win?" Wyatt asked as he racked again.

The juke box stopped and the voices from the bar became clear. Don, who sat at the end of the bar nearest the door to the pool room, was conducting a survey. How many of them, he wanted to know, had a name for their genitals? No one answered. He volunteered that he called his own apparatus Big Luther. Still no answers.

"Billy? I'm willing to bet you got a name for it."

"I do."

"Jack?"

"Yeah, I got a name for it."

Don sold burglar alarms for a living and had always struck Wyatt and Jay as a bit better educated than the others at Belize. Now Don smiled as he got every man but one to admit that he had a name for it. But of the seven women at the bar, only one, Big Faye, admitted that she had given herself a name.

Faye was a large, severe looking woman with short, sandy hair who came to Belize every night after work and drank until about nine, when she weaved toward her car and drove home. Depending on how recently she'd been dumped by yet another man, Faye either drank Pearl Light beer and joked with the others, or she drank Jack Daniels and Coke and sat by herself, pouring out quarters for the saddest C&W songs on the jukebox.

"Whatta you call it?" Don pressed.

"I ain't saying."

Don was short and barrel-chested and sat hunched over the bar, peeling the label of his bottle with his thumbnail as he watched Faye, who sat two stools to his right.

"Lemme see. If my name was Faye and I was your size and strength and I had a snapper, I believe I'd call it . . . *Faith*! Or *Hope*."

"Go to hell, Don."

Jay looked at Wyatt, who had just missed a shot. "So, what do you call yours?"

"Pierre. Pierre zee leetle man."

Jay smiled. "A French putz on an Irishman."

"Dare I ask what you call yours?"

"Faith," Jay said. He put the seven in the side, the two in the same side. "Sometimes hope." He ran the six into the far right corner and left himself a shot on the four in the opposite corner. "Once in a great while, I get to call it charity." He banked the eight into the side where Wyatt was standing. "But more often than not, that's what I end up calling hers."

WHEN JAY LED seven to two, Wyatt again accused Jay of beating up on him at a time when he needed sympathy. Jay scratched on the next break, making the score seven to three.

"My tumor's killing me."

"That's what tumors are for," Jay said. He knew Wyatt was in pain, although it was hard to say how much, since one of Wyatt's favorite games was to whine and pretend he was much more fragile than he actually was. If he really was in pain, Jay decided, he'd be trying not to show it.

"Don't forget that we have to do my taxes before the night's over," Jay added.

Wyatt looked at him. "What's the big rush? You have another week. It's almost as if you're trying to get it done before I go in for my surgery."

"That's right."

"Seems a little self-centered."

Jay smirked. "Is there something different about that?"

Wyatt lined up his break. "Not in the least. That's why I wanted your company tonight. I wouldn't want anyone grovelling with me. Personally, I like a little abuse the night before surgery."

"I know."

They grinned at each other. Wyatt broke. The balls didn't move with the same velocity that Jay gave them, but two solids dropped anyway.

"I'd just like to have the taxes out of the way in case you die or something. By the way, are you ready for death?"

"No."

"That must mean you're ready for another Diet Sprite."

"Since you put it like that, I'll have a Johnny Walker Red on the rocks."

"I like the logic." As Jay stood at the bar, he thought of all the people Wyatt could have spent the evening with, not the least of whom was Sylvia. But Sylvia would have doted and worried, and Wyatt didn't like that. There was Joe, Wyatt's tennis buddy; but Joe would have parked himself in front of the TV and fallen asleep watching ESPN. There was Elizabeth, Wyatt's most serious girlfriend in recent years. Since their breakup they had become friends. But Liz would have probably brought along one of her psychological board games, and Wyatt, too polite to admit that he hated board games, would have been antsy and miserable.

Besides, they were all avoiders. They would have all been stealing glances toward the area of Wyatt's collarbone but pretending that no tumor existed. Jay assumed that Wyatt didn't want to avoid things tonight.

He noticed Jamie Salver sitting at the bar. That made him think about old Nick the Grik. Nick was no avoider, Jay thought. None of these people were avoiders. It came clear to him why Wyatt had wanted to come here tonight, even though he pretended not to.

When he carried the drinks back, he found Wyatt sitting at one of the small tables in the pool room. "Hey. You. No brooding allowed."

"What makes you think I'm brooding?"

"Just a wild guess."

Wyatt reached in his pocket and handed Jay a folded slip of paper. "Just in case."

"Ah, yes. The next of kin. So. You *are* ready to die."

"I wouldn't put it that way."

"Have you thought about what you'll do if you die?"

"What a ridiculous question."

"Let me rephrase it. What if they say the tumor's a bad one and you have six months?"

"I'm not sure I want to talk about this the night before I get the knife."

Jay clinked his beer bottle against Wyatt's glass, which still sat on the table. "Sure you do. What better time?"

Wyatt swayed slightly with the sigh and smirk that broke at the same time. "You're right. As usual."

They studied each other a moment. "Let me rephrase the question yet again. What are *we* going to do if the news is bad. I don't want you thinking you're in this alone."

JAY WON TEN games to five. As they stood at the bar to settle up, Jay, to Wyatt's extreme discomfort, announced that the city's next white mayor would have surgery the following day.

"Damn you," Wyatt hissed.

"Mr. Standish's campaign will suffer a mighty blow if he croaks tomorrow," Jay told them. "Let's take up a small collection right now to show him our support. It'll be a great morale builder."

"You better hope you don't get no nigger doctor cutting on you," said Billy.

"What if you had a black doctor?" Wyatt asked. "What if they wheeled you into the operating room and the last thing you saw before you went under was that your surgeon was black? What would you do?"

"I'd hope to die before he could get his knife out."

"Now, an operating room is not a dark alley, Billy."

Wyatt noticed that everyone was listening. His blood ran a little faster, knowing that he was being stared at by people whose core value he was questioning.

"You know, Billy, I used to think you were a racist."

Billy smiled proudly. "I am." He glanced around the room for approval. The others murmured and guffawed.

"No, you're not. You don't hate blacks. I've seen how you treat that old black man who comes in every morning to sweep up. You're pretty decent to him. You just hate blacks who are more successful than you."

Billy's face went hard, and the room went silent again. "What the fuck you talking about?"

Jay felt the potential for hatred accumulate in the tight moments that followed. He'd never truly felt that he and Wyatt were anything but outsiders. Then Wyatt smiled.

"And that's exactly why I'm running for mayor. To prove to all of you that a white man can still be successful. Just like all of you."

The tension eased. Don raised a glass and insisted on buying Wyatt a drink. Wyatt accepted another Scotch. They all cheered.

"I'm conducting a survey—"

"Yes. I do. I call it Ulysses the Useful."

Don broke an even bigger smile. "I like it. Practical. No bragging. I like it a lot."

On the way out the door, Wyatt gave Jay a hard nudge. "By the way, asshole, your tax forms are already filled out. All you have to do is sign them, Xerox them, and mail them."

"You're a hell of a guy."

In the small, dark passageway between Belize and the empty building next door, they heard a raspy voice.

"Who's that?"

"Me. Nick." The bent figure came toward them, one hand raised.

"Ti-kan-eze," Jay said. "How you doing?"

Nick held up a wobbly hand in a so-so gesture. "Not too good. I had an operation last week. Didn't go too good."

Wyatt and Jay looked at each other. "Sorry to hear that," Wyatt said. "Anything we can do for you?"

"No. Not really. Just tell me, is Jamie in there?"

"She was a little while ago," Jay said. "I didn't notice on the way out."

"She with anybody?"

"No."

"She don't know about my operation." Nick's voice shook a little and he coughed once. "None a them in there knows. They probably think I just disappeared. I didn't tell none of them I was even going in the hospital. Don't y'all tell nobody, okay?"

"Won't tell a soul, Nick."

Jay and Wyatt looked at each other. They knew much about old Nick. He'd come to the States by himself when he was ten, stayed with an uncle who died less than a year later, then supported himself selling newspapers, carrying golf bags, running messages for bookies, picking cotton on the farms just outside of town. When he was sixteen he got a job driving a taxi and did that for forty years. For the next twenty years after that he drove a truck for a beer distributor until they made him retire. He'd outlasted everyone—his wife, three of his four sons. The last surviving son, who was sixty, had never been able to hold a job and depended on Nick for everything, including food and rent money.

"Don't tell nobody you saw me here neither," Nick said.

"We sure won't."

"Especially Jamie. She says I try to spy on her. I ain't spying. I just wonder sometimes if she . . . you know, already forgot about me."

"I don't see how the hell she could," Jay said. "Even *I* can't forget you and I can forget just about anybody."

Nick smiled and filled his skinny iron fist with Jay's hand.

THEY DROVE IN separate cars—Wyatt in his BMW, Jay in his old Chevy, which had a hole in the muffler. Wyatt lived in a new condo about ten miles outside of town. They arrived together. Once inside the apartment, Wyatt started to listen to his messages but turned the machine off before the first message started.

"Ten to five," Jay smiled.

"Bear in mind that you beat me no more than twenty-five percent of the time."

"Ten to five..."

Wyatt opened the refrigerator and brought out ham, cheese, French rolls, four kinds of mustard.

"I thought you weren't allowed to eat the night before surgery," Jay said.

"I'm not. You can."

"You think I'd eat in front of you when you can't?"

"Yes."

"You're right. I would. And I will."

Jay made a sandwich. Wyatt watched, feeling no desire for food.

"So," Jay said. "We never did decide what we'll do if the news tomorrow is bad."

Wyatt threw his hands up. "Can't you give it a rest?"

"This is important."

"What if I don't want to talk about it?"

"I'd agree if this were an abstract notion," Jay said, "but this is the real thing. You stand a chance—small, I know, but a chance—of kicking off when they start pumping in the anesthetic. I know you don't believe in an afterlife, so these may be your last few hours. How do you feel about that? Any plans?"

"Plans? Yeah, if I die, I plan to die."

"What I really mean is what if you make it through the surgery but the biopsy is bad news? What's the program?"

Wyatt got up and paced. Jay watched.

"How about this? We quit our jobs, get on a plane for Scotland, and play golf all the way around the world. If we get back to the States before I die, we head back out again, only shooting pool this time."

"What about your mother?"

"Take her along, too."

Jay nodded a long time, his face grim. "Good plan. Needs some fine-tuning, but I like the general idea."

"Good. Now, can we talk about something else?"

They talked until two, when Wyatt's eyes began to glaze over. Jay slept in the guest room. Wyatt fell asleep quickly but awoke after an hour and worried away the rest of the night. Jay slept all night and awoke when his dreaming mind thought it smelled coffee. By the time Jay had showered and dressed, Wyatt had read the entire newspaper and looked over Jay's tax forms one last time.

"Good morning."

"Good for you, maybe."

"Naw, good for both of us. You're going to breeze in there, pop that little tumor out, and be raring to get back to the pool table so I can thrash you again."

"You seem to have changed attitudes during the night."

"Attitudes are like underwear. You feel better if you change them everyday." Jay nodded toward a small valise on a chair by the table. "I thought it was outpatient surgery."

"Just in case."

They rode in Jay's Chevy. The muffler seemed loudest when the engine was cold, and Wyatt looked around the wooded condominium court, unembarrassed but curious, nonetheless, as to how many of his neighbors might come to their windows to see what was making the noise. As they drove, they talked about the Ravel piano concerto they'd heard on the radio the night before. They agreed that Ravel, despite being a Frenchman, was a pretty damned good composer.

"You seem cheerful for a man who might be dying," Jay said as they pulled up to the hospital entrance.

"Hey, I've got my life figured out. I'm a free man. I'll call you when they're done carving me up."

JAY FOUND HIMSELF unable to concentrate on his work. He spent the morning in his tight cubicle watching the clock, speculating on what might be in progress inside the hospital at that moment. He began to wish that he'd taken the day off, after all, but he didn't want to appear to react in any way to Wyatt's surgery. All morning, the image of Wyatt as he lay stretched out on the operating table unnerved Jay as he drank three times his normal amount of coffee. By ten o'clock he was hopelessly buzzed from the caffeine and got up to pace around the office and bother his coworkers. At ten thirty-six he began to feel nauseated and went to sit in the bathroom. The prospect of life without his best friend finally made him vomit. He felt a little better after that and went back to his cubicle to wait for Wyatt's phone call. The minutes bumped along until eleven fifty-three.

Wyatt's voice was weak, as if he were calling from another country. "Come get me."

When Jay pulled up in front of the hospital, two stout black nurse's aides wheeled Wyatt out the door in a chair, then maneuvered him into the front seat of the Chevy. His dressing was visible under his collar, and Wyatt, pale as his bandages, seemed stiff enough to snap in half.

"It was the damndest thing." Wyatt's voice was weak but steady. "The doc said it was a tiny piece of shrapnel or some such thing. I guess I got hit during the war and didn't even know it."

"You'll be sending off for your Purple Heart?"

"You bet. God . . . I had the strangest dream or vision or hallucination or whatever. I kept thinking the doctor looked like *you*. I think I even screamed at one point." Wyatt looked outside the car. "Where are we going? Expressway's the opposite direction."

"I thought we'd just swing by Belize for a quick game."

"Jay, for Christ's sake . . . "

"I'll let you win this time. I promise."

"Jay, I can't stand up."

"I'll hold you. One game."

"Take me home."

But Jay's blood was on the rise now. He turned the last corner and raced toward the small parking lot beside the bar.

"I'll rack them, you set the cue on the edge of the table and just give it enough of a poke to hit the balls. And we'll leave. We'll be able to say that Wyatt Cobb, man of shrapnel that he is, got up from the operating table and *demanded* a game of pool."

"The fact that it's untrue doesn't seem to bother you."

Jay pulled in, but Billy's pickup was not there. The black metal security bars remained locked across the door.

"There," Wyatt said. "You see. Now take me home."

"He'll be here any minute."

Wyatt sagged back against the head rest. "I'm not up for being bigger than life today, Jay. And I can't get out and call a cab. Just—"

"Wait. Here he is."

Billy pulled in beside them and nodded, his eyes on Wyatt as he lumbered toward the Chevy.

"How's Mr. Standish doing? I see they cut him already."

"He bad wants to shoot a little pool, Billy. But I'm not sure he's up to it."

"He don't look too good."

"Don't let that fool you. Fighter pilot over in Nam."

"Zat so? I didn't know that." Billy winked at Jay and went to open the door. "Come on in."

Wyatt didn't move. He thought about how he had planned to spend the afternoon. Sylvia would come over and read to him while he dozed. Then she'd feed him some of her homemade chicken soup when he woke up and felt like eating.

"Jay, I told Sylvia I'd be home by noon."

"Oh? A little post-surgery date you forgot to mention?"

"Call it whatever you want."

"The stuff of legends, my friend. Had to hurry home from surgery to get laid. Mr. Nick would be proud of you."

"Oh God . . "

Jay backed into the street. "Well, at least we can say that when we left the hospital we headed straight to Belize."

"*You* can say anything you want. I'll say I was sicker than a dead leper and couldn't wait to get home and into my own bed." When Wyatt opened his eyes he felt almost alert. "Besides, I don't believe for a second you would have let me beat you."

The Presto

GENEVA HADN'T HEARD from Nick in over five years, but
when he called at four-thirty in the morning and asked her to work
for a day, he caught her off guard, and her sleepy impulse was to say yes.
There was no small talk about what they had been doing since they last
saw each other. Only Nick's brief statement of his needs for the day.

"Dimitri is sick," Nick began, "my backup cook is in jail. I been on
the phone an hour trying to find somebody."

In the twenty-five years she had known Nick, Geneva had never
refused him anything. Nor had he refused her anything; she had simply
made it a point never to ask him for anything that Nick would have to
refuse.

She put on her glasses to look at the clock. His Greek accent, so
familiar for so long, made her smile. She remembered that his hair was
starting to turn white the last time she saw him, and she wondered if it
was completely white yet. She wondered about that disarming flash in his
smile that always made her want him, no matter where they were. Now
she wished that he'd called just to say hello, the way he used to, in the
middle of the night.

She began to feel uneasy talking to Nick. They had always had an
amusingly adaptive relationship—friends, lovers, coworkers, boss/em-
ployee—their interaction metamorphosing as the moment demanded.
For too many years Geneva had allowed Nick to be the focus of her life,
even though she knew they had no future together. She wasn't sure she
wanted to reopen the attic of discarded feelings that his call had already
evoked.

"Why don't *you* do it?" she asked.

"Hey. I've fried my last ass in a restaurant kitchen. Whadda you think I did with about twenty years of my life?" He paused. "If you can't work, I'll just close for the day."

"Do you still open at five?"

"Yeah. Avis opens up."

Geneva had meant to ask if Avis, the head waitress, still worked for Nick. That might have been reason to refuse him, but now it was too late to say no.

"I'll be in sooner or later," he said. "I got a bunch of errands."

As Geneva dressed, she wondered if she should wear makeup. Nick hated makeup, but she had gotten into the habit of using a little eye shadow and rouge because she saw that it offset her natural pallor. It would also be a good way of demonstrating her independence from Nick. Her hair was still mostly black, and she wore it nearly shoulder-length, flipped under at the bottom. She would wear contact lenses instead of glasses, although Nick had always claimed he liked a woman in glasses. Geneva was still slim but no longer taut. The ten pounds she had gained in the last five years were evenly distributed on her tall frame rather than lumped around her hips. She debated whether she should wear a white kitchen uniform or a navy skirt with a print blouse and flats. She opted for the latter; a uniform would imply that she was the same Geneva that Nick had dumped. She wasn't the same at all, not in her own estimation. She owned her own business, one of the most successful catering enterprises in Mobile, she owned a house, had put her daughter through junior college and her son through trade school. And she had paid cash for her car. She had learned to survive nicely without Nick.

THE PRESTO WAS a small restaurant on Dauphin Street, a few blocks from the State Docks. You couldn't see the harbor but you could smell it and hear it. The Presto had always been a late-night hangout for cabbies, bookies, and Mobile's few hookers. With fourteen stools at the counter and ten booths along the wall, The Presto's only distinction was that it was open at least until midnight and therefore usually crowded, the juke box blasting out Ray Charles, Merle Haggard, Conway and Loretta. It was always lively—sometimes too lively—and even Nick was surprised at how much money he made.

Early in the morning, the place was as quiet as it was noisy at night. By the time Geneva arrived, Avis had opened up, and a few customers sat at the counter and in several booths sipping coffee, eating eggs and grits. Avis stood in the kitchen door smoking a cigarette. The only sound was that of sizzling eggs on the grill behind her.

"Well, look at what the cat drug in," Avis said. She was over six feet tall, even in her tennis shoes. With her short, fox-red hair and thick neck, Avis looked like a guard at a women's prison. Avis's lids seemed weighted down with eye shadow, and her mouth was a thin, bright red oval that sucked on a cigarette.

Geneva glanced around at the mirrored walls and the cigarette burns on the Formica counter and booth tables. Not an atom of the place had changed since she last saw it. She slipped past Avis into the kitchen without looking directly at her and without smiling. The sound of the eggs and bacon on the griddle seemed almost deafening.

"Busy already, huh?"

Avis smirked. "Nothing I can't handle."

Now Geneva did smile. Her distaste for Avis was almost like an old, familiar pair of shoes. Geneva had not stopped hating Avis, merely forgotten her. It felt invigorating to hate her in person again.

Dirty dishes from the night before were stacked beside the dishwashing machine and along the work board in front of the steam table. The dish tubs were empty and dry.

"Where's the dishwasher?" Geneva asked.

"I fired his sorry black ass. Showed up drunk. Again."

"Should have let him wash last night's dishes first."

"He couldn't even see a dish. Some bum will be by looking for day work. If not, you and me can handle it."

Geneva tied on an apron that she found hanging by the sink. Avis went out front to wait on her customers. Geneva turned on the taps to fill the dishwasher tubs, and the water blasted against the stainless steel with the racket of a chain saw. She shook three cups of soap powder into one tub; as the water foamed up blue and cottony, the noise hushed. She would fill the tubs, but she would not wash dishes, she promised herself. Not when it was someone else who had fired the dishwasher.

Geneva propped open the back door and turned on the big fan that sucked the smell of bacon and fresh rolls out of the kitchen and mixed it imperfectly with the garbage can odor of the alley, allowing one scent to alternate with the other.

Without being obvious about it, Geneva watched Avis. She's gained a lot of weight, Geneva noted with satisfaction, looking at Avis's widened rump and straight ankles that plunged tightly into her white tennis shoes. Geneva noticed that Avis still waited on the blacks last.

The place was starting to fill up with customers, and Geneva found herself working with the quick, automatic moves she had mastered many years ago. She slid the orders of eggs and meat onto plates and garnished them with parsley sprigs and orange slices.

"Omelette and grits," Avis hollered, as she picked up the plates Geneva had fixed for her. After she delivered the orders, and clipped more order tickets to the wire line above the grill, she began stacking dirty dishes in the rubber racks for the dishwasher. When Geneva flipped the dishwasher switch, the whirring, sloshing noise filled the kitchen, drowning out the sounds from the grill and fan.

"Don't mind me if I feel good," Avis announced, her big red lips puffed in a smile. "I won the trifecta last night."

"Congratulations," Geneva said dryly.

"Boss won it, too. Two hundred and twenty-six bucks. I ain't told him yet. He don't care anyway."

"He still plays the puppies, huh?"

"The boss?" Avis narrowed her eyes as if it might make her look more privy to inside information. "He plays 'em to be sociable. Wealthy men gamble to be sociable. He don't care if he wins or loses."

Geneva scraped the griddle with the edge of the spatula, then wiped the griddle with a rag. She cracked two more eggs onto the hot surface and watched the way they whitened before she shook the shells empty.

"Now take me," Avis said. "I play 'em to win."

"Good for you. Don't spend it all in one place."

Avis turned on her squeaky soles and went back out front. It was going to be a long day, Geneva decided. At least Avis would be leaving after lunch. Perhaps by then Nick would be in. Maybe they could get reacquainted.

"The only person I know who gambles so he can lose," Avis called into the kitchen from out front, "is Dimitri. He loves to brag about how much he lost at the track."

Dimitri was Nick's oldest son, officially the manager of The Presto. Dimitri was a handsome, fun-loving guy who had always been too friendly to Geneva. She figured he must be twenty-nine or thirty by now. Yes, he was twenty-two years younger than Nick and wasn't Nick fifty-two? She was sure he was. At forty-one, Geneva was eleven years younger than Nick and eleven years older than Dimitri. Nothing serious had ever happened between Geneva and Dimitri, but a rumor had started that Dimitri and Geneva had something going. Nick refused to believe her when she told him it wasn't true. That was the reason they had gone their own ways five years ago. Geneva was too proud to beg Nick to believe her.

AVIS AND GENEVA didn't talk again until the breakfast rush was over. As the crowd thinned out, Avis collected all the dirty dishes in the restaurant and ran them through the dishwasher. From time to time the old machine clanged and coughed to a halt, then started up again. Each time Avis came into the kitchen with more dishes, Geneva plunged a few more inches into her silence.

"I hate waitin' on niggers," Avis said. "They don't know enough to even leave a tip."

"Give them decent service and maybe they would."

"I just miss the good old days. When they couldn't even come in here," Avis said.

When all the dishes were done, Avis brought two cups of coffee into the kitchen. "Cream with no sugar, right?"

"You have a memory like an elephant," Geneva said.

Avis laughed. "You don't have to finish that sentence."

Geneva allowed herself for the first time that morning to lock onto the eyes that studied her so closely.

"You look pretty good," Avis said.

"Thanks."

Avis was silent as her guarded smile hardened. "I see you ain't going to bother to lie to me about the way *I* look."

"No. I'm not."

Avis laughed again. "Good. That makes you the only honest person left in Mobile. So, you like my restaurant? See how I run it different from them Greeks?"

"Did you say *your* restaurant?"

"Yeah. I pretty much run the show now. Nick don't give a damn about this place no more."

"What about Dimitri?"

"Oh sure, his title is manager, but he lets me run the place the way I think it oughta be run. Nick just comes by to pick up the money. That is, what money there is after these sluts he calls waitresses are done clipping him."

"I heard there was a lot of turnover."

Avis shrugged, trying to appear callous. "They get caught stealing, they get fired. It's simple." Avis let a smile slowly break. "So you *do* keep up with this place."

Geneva deepened the lie a little more. She no longer had any stake in Nick and therefore nothing to lose if Nick found out she had lied to Avis.

"Just what I hear from Nick," she said.

Avis's smile flickered back to neutral. "Oh? He told me he ain't seen you in years."

"Maybe he doesn't want you to know everything he does."

Although Avis's smile did not change, Geneva felt a rise in the heat of the gaze.

Geneva's heart flooded and pounded as she devised her next lie. She told herself that Avis was not worth lying to, even if the lies could somehow devastate the woman. But something about Avis had often caused Geneva over the years to do and say things she had not planned on.

"If you want to know the truth," Geneva said calmly, "Nick thinks *you're* the one who's clipping him."

Avis's eyes opened wide for a moment, then quickly narrowed again. "You're lying. He never said that."

Geneva finally looked away.

"That rotten Greek son of a bitch." Avis left the kitchen, fishing in her apron pocket for a dime as she headed toward the pay phone at the back of the restaurant.

Geneva sipped her coffee. She hadn't expected that Avis might cry.

DURING THE remainder of the morning, Avis was either at the phone dialing furiously or else sitting at the counter drinking one cup of coffee after another. Geneva stayed in the kitchen waiting for Avis to finally make contact with Nick, at which time Geneva planned to leave.

A man came in and sat at the counter. Avis ignored him.

"You have a customer," Geneva said.

Avis briefly looked up. Her eyes were puffy and her makeup had streaked down her cheeks. "Piss on him."

The customer sensed that something was going on and left. Avis made at least twenty-five trips to the phone, Geneva guessed, and each time returned to the counter. She had quit drinking coffee and now just stared out the window at the street.

Geneva was filing her nails when Avis came into the kitchen, took a large steak from the refrigerator and threw it on the grill. The tears had dried and now her jaws were clamped together with rage.

"If he thinks I'm clipping him, he ain't seen nothing."

"Oh, so you *have* been clipping him?"

Avis leveled her hard eyes at Geneva, and Geneva doled the look right back.

"You still think I'm the one who told Nick about you and Dimitri, don't you?"

"Well . . . ?"

"It was Dimitri that told him. He got drunk one night and Nick slugged him. Dimitri knew he couldn't hit his own father, so he told him that to hurt him."

Geneva shook her head. "I don't think I'll be buying that one, but thank you."

"I ain't never had nothing against you, Geneva. In fact, I even like you."

Geneva laughed. "Oh? Since when?"

Avis jammed a fork into the steak and flipped it, sending licks of fire hissing up around the sides.

"I dunno. Maybe just since this morning."

Geneva's contempt filled her throat. "Well, I'm flattered." She watched Avis poke furiously at the steak. "But it seems to me he's been pretty good to you over the years."

"My ass! He don't remember when you do him a favor. You oughta know that as good as anybody."

Geneva's mind quickly sorted through her own list of unpaid favors, a list she had tried to discard along with everything else about Nick.

"I pulled his ass drunk and half-drowned out of his swimming pool one night," Avis said, her voice rising. "And what do I get? He calls me a thief! A fuckin thief!"

Geneva didn't hear a word after swimming pool. What was this two-cent bitch ever doing at Nick's house, in Nick's swimming pool? Geneva had never, in twenty years, been to Nick's house. Nick had never invited her, and she had never asked to go. Not even after Dolores died. The mistress must never visit the man's home, Nick had told her once. It was part of Greek culture. "We're not in Greece," Geneva told him, but he only smiled. She accepted that rule as long as Dolores was alive, but after Dolores was gone, Geneva had thought Nick might invite her home with him some night. At least once.

"I think that steak is done," Geneva said. "Unless you were trying to cremate it."

Avis speared it with her fork and slapped it onto a platter, the grease spattering onto her apron. "I wish I was hungry enough to eat every steak in that ice box."

She took a small vat of battered oysters from the refrigerator and scooped several handfuls of them into a fryolator basket, which she dropped into the fat. The grease bubbled golden over them.

"That two-faced Eye-talian Greek son of a bitch." She left the kitchen abruptly and went to the phone again.

Geneva began peeling potatoes, listening as best she could over the sizzling oysters to hear in case Avis got an answer. But Avis slammed the receiver and stormed back into the kitchen, where she lifted the fryolator basket out of the froth and shook off the grease, then flipped them onto the platter with the steak.

"Eat."

"I'm not hungry," Geneva said.

"Neither am I, but I'm going to eat anyway. I'm gonna eat all the expensive stuff he always said the help couldn't have." She stuffed two oysters into her mouth and talked as she chewed. "I've hated this place since the first day I walked in here. How do you think my kids feel when someone asks them where their momma works and they have to say The Presto? I'll tell you how they feel. Embarrassed."

"Nobody's making you work here, Avis."

"Goddam right." She picked up her platter and carried it out to the counter, where she sat down. Geneva finished peeling potatoes, carrots, and onions, then rummaged through the refrigerator looking for lamb with which she could make a stew. Nick always had some lamb around. Finding none in the kitchen refrigerator, she went down to the cellar to look in the freezer.

As she descended the stairs, she couldn't help but remember the times she and Nick had made love down here, on a pile of dirty linen, or standing up somewhere just out of sight of the stairs in case someone came down. She wondered why she bothered to taunt Avis when she'd long ago convinced herself that Nick did not matter. Then she remembered; it was because Avis claimed to have been at Nick's house.

Geneva found the lamb she was looking for, already cut up for stew.

She brought the plastic bag of lamb chunks up to the kitchen. Avis was grilling another steak.

"That last one made me hungry," she said. "You want some key lime pie?"

"No thanks."

"I just called the health department. They'll shut this place down today. I know the inspector."

"You think Nick doesn't know him, too?"

"I know him better. Before he gets here, I'll go to the Chinese joint down the street and borrow some of their big, black cockroaches."

Geneva studied Avis's huge bosom. Nick had always said, at least to Geneva, that he preferred small breasts.

"When was it exactly that you dragged Nick out of his swimming pool?" Geneva asked.

"I dunno. Six, seven years ago."

"Where was Dolores?"

"In Greece, visiting her folks. His folks. Somebody's folks. I don't remember."

"Where was Dimitri?"

"How the hell should I know?"

Geneva realized Avis was probably lying about having been at Nick's house, and the thought further fanned her anger. She toyed with the idea of asking Avis to describe the place. How many rooms? What kind of furniture? How big was this pool?

"I don't care. I'm quitting this joint. I can get a job at Anthony's or Wentzel's or anywhere I want."

A customer had seated himself at the counter. Avis hollered to him from the kitchen.

"You want a steak? It's free."

The old man nodded, but he glanced around nervously, as if Nick might be hiding someplace, ready to jump out and scold him for eating a stolen steak.

GENEVA'S ANGER began to ebb as she examined her reasons for

disliking Avis. If it was Dimitri, not Avis, who made Nick think he and Geneva were fooling around, there was no reason to hold Avis responsible for Nick's treatment of her. And if Avis was lying about having been at Nick's house, there was no reason to be jealous. Avis had not denied that she was clipping Nick, but that was between Avis and Nick.

As she pondered these things, the lunch rush began. Avis parked herself at the counter with her mountain of food and continued to eat. When she wasn't eating, she was on the phone. Geneva waited on the customers, then went into the kitchen to cook their food. The restaurant filled up quickly, and with service slowed down by Avis's eat-in, customers began to line up at the door. Geneva worked quickly but made sure she did not appear hurried or harried. She wondered why she was working so hard to keep the place running when she should be doing what Avis was doing. Her resentment slowly shifted from Avis to Nick. He was the one who expected everyone to kill themselves for him. He was the one who wanted mistresses, but who set nonnegotiable rules for the relationships.

When she had time, between taking orders and cooking, Geneva collected dirty dishes from the booths and ran them through the washer. And when the line at the cash register blocked the doorway, she took cash. The customers were getting impatient, but Geneva ignored their complaints. She merely looked at them with her quiet half-smile and said, "Are you ready to order now?"

"I only got a half-hour to eat," one of them complained. "I been in here twenty minutes already."

"Then go eat somewheres else," Avis bellowed.

When they heard that, most of the customers left; others left when Geneva told them that most of the menu items were not available because she hadn't made them.

There were dirty dishes everywhere, but Geneva was too tired to deal with them. She went downstairs and looked for something to sit on. She considered breaking open a carton of towels and aprons from the Chinese laundry and spreading them on the floor so she could lay down, but instead she sat on a box of canned fruit and massaged her legs. She decided she must be getting old if she tired so easily. Her lids folded over her eyes and she slipped into a half-sleep, picturing Nick's pool. She had never seen it, and rarely had she even tried to imagine it. But in her dream the pool was oval in shape and lined with light blue tiles. Nick's hat floated on the water, but Nick was nowhere to be seen.

Geneva was jolted awake by the jukebox, and the sound of Avis's voice as she hollered. Then the sudden silence. She guessed that Avis must have unplugged the juke box.

Geneva climbed the stairs and found Avis still seated at the counter. Her plates were mostly empty, and Avis looked a little pale.

"Health inspector come yet?" Geneva asked.

"He will."

"Did you get those Chinese cockroaches."

Avis gave Geneva a hard look but said nothing.

Geneva went into the kitchen. There were dirty dishes everywhere, and with the back door open, the place swarmed with flies. She considered leaving everything and going home. If Avis wanted to stay until Nick came by, that was up to her. But as she considered, she also began cleaning up the kitchen. She emptied the dishwasher tubs, cleaned them out, drew fresh water, and began running through all the dirty dishes. An hour later, the dishes were all clean, the grill was scrubbed, and the floor was mopped. Geneva was breaking down the steam table when Avis came into the kitchen, her narrow, puffy eyes knifing.

"You know, something don't quite add up. I'm starting to think Nick never said nothing like that at all. It's just you trying to start some shit, ain't it?"

Geneva scraped at the caked-on layer in the bottom of the grits vat and said nothing.

Avis continued. "You always hated me. And acted like you was better than me. I never could figure that out. I mean, *my* kid got into nursing school, yours didn't. My old man still lives with me and supports me, yours took off years ago. I drive a new Buick, you drive an old Ford."

Geneva chose not to mention that the old Ford was now a new Lincoln. She wanted only to clean the place up and close before the supper rush started. "Just lock that door so we can both get out of here," she said.

"I ain't going nowhere until you tell me the truth. Did Nick really say I was clipping him?"

Geneva faced her. "Well, aren't you?"

"Did *he* say it?"

"Did you really drag him out of his pool?"

Avis's eyes always told more than her mouth, Geneva remembered, and her eyes were almost always ready to lie.

"Yes," Avis said.

Geneva didn't want to believe her and therefore didn't. She became angry at herself for letting things that had ended five years ago flare up in her life again.

She started toward the door to lock it, but Avis grabbed her arm.

"Did he say I was clipping him or not?"

Geneva saw three people coming into the door. "Let's just lock up so we can both get out of here."

"Answer me first."

Geneva's heart raced as she realized that she and Avis might finally come to blows. Avis was bigger, but Geneva felt that her own hatred was the more fervid and therefore likely to give her more strength. The two women stood inches apart, staring. Geneva's muscles tightened. More people were coming into the restaurant and Geneva felt them as they all watched.

"I'll take Avis in two rounds," one of the customers said. Several others laughed. Avis let go of Geneva, grabbed a half-full cup of coffee from the counter and heaved it. The cup shattered against the wall, just above one customer's head. A large chunk of mirror broke off from the wall and slid onto a table. The customers scrambled toward the door while Avis continued to heave coffee cups and plates at them.

SHE RECOGNIZED him by the way he coasted along the curb to the No Parking sign and sat there idling a moment before he turned the engine off and got out. To her dismay, all her old reactions to him—the short breath, dry throat, fuzzy vision, the ringing in her ears, and pulsing in the back of her neck—returned the instant she became aware of him. She found herself frozen, unable to move or avert her eyes from his as he watched her through the window.

He was never hurried in his movements. The car door closed as if it had been nudged shut by a gentle wind. Nick looked older and a little heavier. His hair was pure white and his eyes seemed softer, less steely than they used to. The fact that he wore casual slacks and a golf shirt also made him seem more mellow. He stepped aside to let the departing customers by, holding the door for them.

He nodded at Geneva. "How have you been?"

"All right."

Avis hurled her restaurant key on the floor as she screamed into his face. "You can take this dump and stick half of it up your ass and the other half up hers." Avis blasted out the door and ran down the street.

Geneva watched him. He seemed much less sure of himself than in the past, and she found that refreshing in a man whose sureness about everything left little room for anyone else's. "Next time you have to run somebody off, do it yourself."

He glanced away. Shyness was a new quality in Nick, Geneva thought. It was almost charming. His eyes wandered toward the street then back to Geneva.

"I've tried to. She don't take it serious when I fire her. I fired her again last night, and she was here to open up this morning at four-thirty. When I drove by and saw her here, that's when I decided the only way to get rid of her was to call you."

Geneva said nothing. She remembered the exertion of the day, and although it now seemed distant and unreal, her feet ached and her knees and shoulders were tight with fatigue.

Nick flipped the sign in the window to Closed, then he locked the restaurant and walked Geneva toward her car.

"White Lincoln? You must be doing all right."

The dry throat and pulsing neck returned in an instant. She wished she no longer felt anything for him, or that he no longer felt anything for her. In spite of his age and the obvious mellowing, he was, to her, still the immigrant boy who had come here alone at fourteen, lied about his age to get into the army so he could see a war, worked his way to the top at one of Mobile's best restaurants, and saved every spare dime to buy The Presto and its late-night, riffraff clientele, never doubting his ability to subdue even the meanest drunk. They didn't make them like Nick anymore.

"I need to get home," she said.

The pause was longer this time, and Geneva thought she saw something akin to pain in his eyes. He tried to cover it quickly with a laugh.

"Yeah. Long day." He reached in his pocket and took out a roll of money. He pulled off a one hundred dollar bill and held it toward her.

"Make it three. You cost me a whole day's business."

He seemed surprised but hurried to accommodate her. She put the money in her pocket and sighed. "Well. I'm glad I saw you. I was wondering how you were getting along."

"I'll call you tomorrow," he said.

"I'd rather you didn't."

The pain snuck up on him too quickly this time, and his eyes glistened in the moment before he could look away. She had never loved him more than in that moment, she thought.

"Okay. I understand. I guess. Thanks again."

She got in her car, knowing she should leave before she weakened. As she pulled away, she saw him in her rearview mirror watching her. To distract herself from the emptiness that had suddenly sprung up inside her, she tried to picture her bathtub full of hot water and how good it would feel on her neck and chin and shoulders as she stretched out.

Only when she had rounded a corner did she allow herself to cry, but to her surprise, the tears that had felt so near all day had dried up somewhere on their way to her eyes.

A Three-Martini Lunch

S ORROWFUL JONES had told his advertising agent to meet him
for lunch at The Taco Shell, Clanton's new Mexican restaurant. The
Taco Shell was a small white stucco building that stood almost in the
shadow of the town's other recent addition, the million-dollar peach
monument, which had been built to announce Clanton's status as
capitol of the Chilton County peach growing industry. Sorrowful had
invited Ed to lunch at The Taco Shell instead of some other place because
he knew the very sight of the gaudy, one hundred-foot high statue
angered Ed Proctor, Clanton's only advertising agent, since the town had
hired an agency in Birmingham rather than Ed Proctor Images to design
the thing. Sorrowful knew the sight of the monument filled Ed not only
with anger but also with a haunting sense of inadequacy, which was
exactly how Sorrowful wanted Ed to feel. Ed was not listening to his top
client anymore, and Sorrowful had been reminding himself for the last
two months that *he*, not Ed, was the one writing the checks, and from
now on he, not Ed, was the one who would call the shots.

Sorrowful had rehearsed his speech every time he drove alone in one
of his cars, so he knew all the things he wanted to say. He could deliver
the speech from memory in exactly eighty seconds, provided Ed could
keep his mouth shut that long. Sorrowful had timed himself. If there was
one thing he'd learned from his twenty-one years of working with Ed, it
was how to time a speech to the second.

Carlos Bandana, Clanton's most ethnic resident, stood with dignity
in his stiff white shirt, black bow tie, and black tux trousers as Sorrowful
walked in. Carlos held a basket of corn chips in one hand, a bowl of salsa

in the other, and several plastic-coated menus under his arm. Carlos was about fifty, Sorrowful guessed, a dressed-up peasant, like the guys on those postcards Sorrowful had sent everybody from Cancun, when he and Myrtle went down there on their one foreign vacation a few years back.

"Welcome to Carlos Bandana's Taco Shell. I am Carlos Bandana. Lunch for one?"

"Carlos Banana?"

"Carlos Ban*dana*. Lunch for one? "

"Two. What kind of car you drive, that VW out there?"

"Si, Senor."

"You and me need to talk about getting you into a new *ride*, Fella."

"Si, Senor. Haha, haha; I see your TV publicities. You must always be trying to sell the car. Smoking section or no smoking?"

"Smoking. My late friend is one of those pack-an-hour types. Better put us under one of them ceiling fans."

"Si, Senor. And to drink?"

"Nothing. Thanks."

Carlos set the chips and salsa on the table. "Not even a glass of water?"

"I guess you *are* new. You ain't noticed that the water around here tastes like a grade school chalkboard?"

Carlos smiled for the first time. "This is why I put a large slice of lime in each glass of water."

Sorrowful thought a moment and changed his mind. "I don't usually drink, but today I might just need me a little bracer. What cha got good?"

"Specialty of the house is marga*ri*ta."

"I always wanted to try a martini. You got one a them?"

"Si, Senor. I make the perfect dry martini."

"Is that better than a wet one?"

"Si, Senor. Much better."

"Well, bring it on. They come with an olive, right?"

"Si, Senor."

"Bring me a bunch. I love olives."

When Carlos had left, Sorrowful rehearsed his speech once more, then got up from his booth and paced. He ended up at the door that faced out into the empty parking lot. His vast stomach alternately growled and begged. He'd been too nervous to eat breakfast that morning, and now that it was time to deliver the speech he'd been planning for weeks now, he felt tense in his jawbone and neck, unsure of the exact order of the points he wanted to make. The sweat had already collected in the many creases of his perpetually sunburned face and was draining into the sparse but wiry strands of the beard Ed had talked him into growing for the new ad campaign.

Carlos brought the small martini glass on a large tray.

"My martini is famous throughout the Caribbean," he said. "I was once the bartender on a Royal Caribbean liner."

"That's just great." Sorrowful took the glass from the tray and held it up for a close look. He counted five olives in the bottom of the glass, then sipped.

"Does el Senor Jones agree that my martini is the most very excellent?"

"Best I ever had. No doubt about it."

Carlos bowed and retreated again. Sorrowful took another sip and told himself that for all his distaste for confrontation and all Ed's love of it, Sorrowful was going to stand his ground this time and do what he knew he had to do. He glanced around to make sure Carlos wasn't watching, then fingered two olives into his mouth. Yes, quite good, he decided, and took a mouthful of the martini. It moved in two directions at the same time: down onto his empty stomach and up into his turgid brain. He fingered out two more olives and swallowed the rest of the martini in a single tilt. He was about to retake control of his business.

Sorrowful remembered his favorite line from his favorite movie. "Ain't life grand," he said aloud.

Carlos appeared as if through the wall. "Does El Senor Jones desire another martini?"

"Yeah. It was good. Just put a few more olives in it, will you?" While he waited for the second drink, Sorrowful tasted a corn chip with a dab of salsa on it. Too hot. Way too hot. Besides, it didn't go with the martini taste in his mouth. Or was it olives he was tasting, he wondered.

By the time Ed showed up, Sorrowful had been to the bathroom, paced around the empty restaurant a bit more, and finished his second martini. Sorrowful felt as confident as he'd ever felt, plus a little bit mean as a bonus.

HE SAW ED'S car even before it pulled into the parking lot of Carlos Bandana's Taco Shell. Ed didn't see Sorrowful watching for him because Ed, as Sorrowful had known he would be, was fixated on the giant peach pedestal. Sorrowful had plenty of time to get back to his seat. Carlos, as he had been directed, whisked away Sorrowful's martini glass.

Ed strolled in, looking, as usual, as if he were lost. His shaggy hair was almost down to his shoulders, a mixture of gray, white, and heavy black. Sorrowful thought Ed's hair looked like a larger version of his moustache. Ed's face was even thinner than it was last week, Sorrowful noticed as he studied Ed in the bright light of the door.

It was the sunglasses, Sorrowful now realized. Ed was one of those people whose face was too thin for sunglasses, since they hid most of his face and not just his eyes. Ed's brown leather jacket and seersucker slacks struck Sorrowful as nothing short of ridiculous.

Ed was talking with Carlos, acting as if he'd forgotten why he was even there. Carlos pointed. Ed jerked once and started toward Sorrowful. He abruptly slid into the booth.

"You're late."

"Yeah." Ed neither smiled nor apologized. He grabbed a menu and scanned it too fast to read anything. He lay the menu on the table then slid his sunglasses to the end of his nose and looked at Sorrowful over the rims. "So, what's up? How ya been? Business any better?"

"No."

"Well, buy more spots."

"We're running twice as many spots as we used to and getting a quarter of the business."

Ed slid his glasses all the way off, folded them and tucked them in his jacket pocket, never taking his hawkish eyes from Sorrowful's face.

"Oh. Now I see why we're here. It's the Blame Ed Show. Okay, if that's the program, have at it."

Carlos came to the table. His smile vanished when he saw Ed's agitation. "Something to drink for the Senors?"

"I'll have a martini," Sorrowful smiled to Carlos. "And could you put lots of olives in it please?"

"Si, Senor. And for Senor?"

"Sure," Ed said. "Martini sounds fine. But *no* olives."

Carlos trotted away. Ed's face contorted in disbelief. "Martini? Winfried, I had no idea."

The first two martinis wafted through Sorrowful in a small crest of confusion. Timing was important here, and it was not yet time to push Ed over the edge. Let him relax first, perhaps even let his defenses all the way down to the point where he might become reasonable. Sorrowful pretended to luxuriate in his position, even as he recognized that he was really postponing the row he had planned. But it was important to put Ed at ease before he launched the attack.

Ed sat hunched over, elbows on the table, hands clasped, head nodding in rhythm to some nonexistent music that only Ed seemed to hear. "Sock it to me, Big Guy. Beat old Ed up before he's even been fed."

"How do you like the place?"

Ed glanced around. "Seems a little too respectable for a *real* Mexican restaurant." He took out his cigarettes, lit one, and blew a steam of smoke from the side of his mouth at an upward angle, away from Sorrowful.

"So, what's up?"

Carlos brought the martinis. Sorrowful knew he had already drunk his limit and that he should take this third martini slowly. Ed smiled when he saw all the olives in Sorrowful's drink.

"Drink up," Sorrowful said.

"Drinking makes me nervous. And so does this joint. We've never had lunch anywhere but Burger King."

"Drink up." He lifted his glass and waited for Ed to lift his. They clinked. Ed took a small sip, Sorrowful a big one. Ed set his glass on the table and began to finger his hair just above the ear, his gesture of maximum stress.

Sorrowful tried to stand up without making it obvious that he was hammered. Carlos approached the table again.

"Which way to the head?" Sorrowful asked.

"Senor?"

"The restroom."

"Thees way."

"Thanks. Get this guy another drink while I'm gone."

"For crying out loud," Ed muttered.

Sorrowful worked hard to walk slowly and steadily. In the men's room, he peered at himself in the mirror, blinking until he found only a single image of himself. His stomach churned and his head spun, so he sat on the commode in the single stall, his arms folded over his knees, his head on his forearms. When he closed his eyes, his head spun again; but when he opened them, the men's room spun. He'd blown it, he told himself. He should have stopped after the first one. Now what he needed to do was eat, sober up, and proceed with his business.

Sorrowful staggered to the sink and splashed water on his face. He looked at himself for a moment, then made his way back to the table. Ed was devouring corn chips and salsa as he pored over the menu. His first martini glass was still nearly full and the second was untouched.

"You ready to order?" he asked, as Sorrowful sat down.

"You don't want to drink and be sociable first?"

Ed's worried look returned. "Damn it, Winfried, why are you acting so strange? First you want to have lunch in a new place, and now you want to drink. I wish to hell you'd just tell me what's on your mind."

Carlos was coming their way. Sorrowful didn't know much about Mexican food, so he let Ed do the ordering. Ed ordered what sounded like enough food for ten people, but Sorrowful didn't care; he just wanted something to eat. He avoided eye contact with Ed so that Ed wouldn't realize how drunk he was. He ate a handful of chips, wondering how Ed could have eaten most of the salsa and still have a voice.

"How's the family?" Ed asked.

Family. Yes. "Fine."

"So, what's up?"

Sorrowful could see no reason to put things off any longer. He sighed, blinked, shrugged. He knew had to talk fast so he wouldn't stammer. "Okay, I invited you to lunch today to fire you. There. Feel better now?"

Ed stared a moment, then swilled down his first martini in a single gulp. He stared another moment at Sorrowful and picked up the second martini. Now Ed's eyes were hot and hard. His discomfort had vanished, and he looked dug-in for combat. It was exactly what Sorrowful had expected.

ED AND SORROWFUL had worked together since Sorrowful opened his lot almost fifteen years ago. Sorrowful was one of Ed's first clients, when Ed left the Atlanta agency he'd been working for and opened his own in Montgomery. Ed came up with the Sorrowful Jones routine one night when his four-year-old walked up to him with a toy car and said, "You can't have this." It got Ed thinking. Minutes later, his wife said that she had nothing to wear to work the next day, and as far as she was concerned she'd look better in a barrel than the clothes she owned. That got Ed thinking even more.

All night long he heard his little boy saying, "You can't *have* this." In weeks, Sorrowful was selling cars faster than he could bring them in from the auctions. He no longer had to worry about his balance when he wrote checks for his monthly bills. Before a year had passed, Sorrowful had no bills, not even a house mortgage, and when he moved his family into a bigger house that had a swimming pool, he paid cash for it. And Sorrowful became a local celebrity. He was generous with his new wealth and contributed to all the charities. He was named chairman of every event from the Chilton County Heart Association Rodeo to the Peach Ball and county fair. Every country-western star or NASCAR driver who appeared at a Clanton event received not only the keys to the city but also a Sorrowful Jones used car, which said star was encouraged to donate to a needy citizen in the area. For almost fifteen years, Sorrowful Jones was the most recognizable figure between Birmingham and Montgomery, and he loved every moment of his notoriety.

But then Ed had to go and ruin it all.

Sorrowful remembered the afternoon a few months earlier when it all started to come apart. It had been raining for a week, but now the weather was about to clear, and Sorrowful expected business to pick back up.

"Let's do that station wagon spot now," Sorrowful said. "I may not have time for it the rest of the week."

Ed took a deep breath. "I don't want to do another spot today." Ed began to pace and lit another cigarette, even though he already had three going in various ashtrays around the studio. "I think we need to change our approach."

"How so?"

"Let's do something . . . something more dignified, I guess. I don't know what the hell I want."

Sorrowful rolled his eyes and cleared his throat. He had noticed a lack of enthusiasm from Ed for several months but had not realized until now what the problem was.

Ed studied Sorrowful carefully. "Maybe something that comes a little closer to portraying the real you."

Sorrowful smiled. "Well, I'm a deacon at my church. We could do a script that goes something like this." Sorrowful summoned his monk expression and spoke in a monotone. "Folks, this here's the Reverend Sorrowful Jones. God asked me to tell you all about these wonderful used cars."

Ed threw his arms up. "No, no, no. You don't get it. You're not going to be *Sorrowful Jones* anymore. Deacon or otherwise. Give me a couple of days to try and come up with something. I'll holler at you. In the meantime, stop thinking of yourself as Sorrowful Jones. Your real name is Winfried Witherspoon. Isn't it? It's been so long I've damned near forgotten."

Sorrowful grimaced. No one had called him Winfried in years. He tried to remember the last person to call him that. He decided it must have been his mother, just before she died.

AS SOON AS Sorrowful left, Ed went to work on a new ad campaign for Winfried Witherspoon's Previously Owned Classic Car Boutique. All of his other clients needed a fresh idea, too, Ed decided. Sales were down for furniture, groceries, and discount fireworks. All of Ed's clients were blaming Ed directly for the sales slump. Ed showed them headlines in *The Wall Street Journal* that said the slump was nationwide, but no one wanted to blame *The Wall Street Journal*. They wanted to blame Ed; and Ed, feeling guilty over what he knew was a gradual slide into apathy, began to blame himself.

Ed worked all night on new concepts for Winfried. By five the next morning, he had six ideas on storyboards. Ed was positive that Winfried would like the new image. Four of the spots were based on the theme of Winfried Witherspoon as a purveyor of fine things; food and wine, furniture, jewelry, and the like. Each spot would finish with Winfried talking about the previously-owned collector cars at his lot. Ed was especially fond of that series. If Sorrowful went for it, Ed would get Winfried onto a weight loss program so that he'd look good in the sporty clothes Ed had in mind for the ads.

In another spot, Ed planned to blow up a front page of *The Wall Street Journal* and have Winfried stand in front of it talking about fine older cars as an investment. Perhaps they could even get some additional photos from the New York Stock Exchange that showed the trading floors. Ed smiled. Maybe they'd actually fly to New York and make their own photos on location. Ed hadn't been to New York in twenty years. It would do him good, he thought, to visit the Mecca of advertising and get an infusion of new ideas. Maybe he could look up a few of his old friends who were in the business there. At the very least, he'd try to look up some of his old friends in the agency business in Atlanta.

Ed worked through the night. At five o'clock, he went out to an all-night restaurant next to the Interstate for breakfast. He felt liberated from a fifteen-year rut of hokey ads for used car lots and cheap furniture stores. Now it was time to add a little class to his act. The only thing that scared Ed was that he hadn't tried anything classy in so long that he was no longer sure he knew what class advertising was. He often ruminated about the fact that his family's cars and clothes had been bought with money earned by insulting the public intelligence.

But once they saw his new advertising style, Ed wouldn't have to ruminate anymore. He knew he was on the verge of a breakthrough in his career, the first since he had left Montgomery and moved to Clanton, and it made the blood pound through his veins as if it were driven by a jack hammer.

"SORROWFUL JONES Used Cars."

Ed smiled. "May I speak to Winfried Jones, connoisseur of the automotive good life."

"I've been wondering if you'd left town or something," Sorrowful said. "When are we going to do this week's TV spots? I've got three or four cars I want to push."

"Come on over this morning," Ed said. "Wear your best suit, and bring a couple of others along, too."

"Suits?"

"Just do it, Winfried. You're going to love your new image. And it's not just an *image*, it's you."

Sorrowful walked in at ten. Ed noticed right away that Winfried did not look enthusiastic.

"This better be good," Sorrowful said.

The first spot featured Sorrowful, off camera, reading a report from a 1971 issue of Car and Driver Magazine about what a great car the 1956 Ford had been, and how it made Lee Iacocca's career. Then the camera came in tight on a 1956 Ford and Sorrowful's narration went on and on about how Winfried Jones still had respect for the great old cars of America, and that's why he was making them available to the good people of Clanton.

"I don't sell 1956 Fords," Sorrowful protested. "Those are classics. I sell clunkers."

The next morning, they shot two more spots, one in which Winfried stood in front of a wall-sized picture of the World Trade Towers and talked about the economics of owning an inexpensive used car, one in good shape, to drive to work, and how that would save wear and tear on your newer car, which could then be saved for special occasions.

In the second spot, Sorrowful droned about how great it was to have been a teenager during the 1950s and how people in Clanton could relive those wonderful days with a vintage car from that splendid era. Winfried wore blue jeans and a black motorcycle jacket. His hair was combed in a ducktail, and he wore sunglasses. While Ed got the camera set up, Sorrowful looked at himself in the mirror.

"This is just plain awful," he said. "I look like a cross between Winston Churchill and a truck tire tread."

"Winfried, you look like you just stepped out of a James Dean movie."

It was the first time that Sorrowful had ever wanted to punch Ed out. He measured the back of Ed's head with the golf club that one of the new ads had him leaning on.

Ed almost caught him but didn't.

THE ENCHILADA platters began to arrive just as Ed was tossing back the last of his second martini. He glared at Sorrowful over the steaming food.

"You've lost your mind. I created you, Winfried. You couldn't survive without me."

"Oh shiiiit, Ed . . ."

"No, those old ads. They *humiliate* us for God's sake. Can't you see that?"

"I don't mind being humiliated as long as I'm rich."

"You got no pride. Not even the unhealthy kind."

Sorrowful tried to summon an expression that would look just as dug-in as Ed's, but he could not capture a single, well defined image of Ed. "We're going back to doing things right, Bubba."

Ed rolled his eyes.

"You got it wrong, Ed. *You're* the damned one that couldn't survive without *me*. Truth is I'm *not* surviving. I used to be rich, but you're doing your damndest to screw that up."

"We're not changing the ads."

Sorrowful sat back, holding Ed's double image in his steady gaze. "That's where you're just flat wrong, Ed. I *am* changing the ads. 'Cause I'm changing ad agencies today."

CARLOS HAD been watching from his bar, where he pretended to wipe glasses with a cotton cloth. Although he looked no more than fifty, Carlos was nearly seventy. He knew he had a bad heart, even though a doctor had never told him so.

Now he snuck the counter phone out of sight and called his waiter, Manuel. "I got trouble from two customers who don't like each other," Carlos whispered.

"I'll be there in ten minutes," Manuel whispered back.

"Bring Fernando, too."

"Right."

Carlos approached the booth with two glasses of water. He hoped to defuse the situation developing in the booth before it got out of hand. In his own experience, two people who glared at each other the way these two did were destined to come to blows.

"You like the food, eh? Is from Guadalajara, ha ha. I bet you never been there?"

Sorrowful and Ed ignored Carlos.

"I own the character of Sorrowful Jones," Ed said. "You don't know this, but I copyrighted the name and the concept over ten years ago."

Carlos went back to the bar. His eyes beat between his customers and the front window, where he watched for Manuel and Fernando.

"You were a bum when I met you," Sorrowful shouted.

"And you were a simpleton. An idiot. And still are!"

"You wouldn't have a pot to piss in without me. We were both doing fine," Sorrowful hammered the table with his fist. "Until you changed the damn ads."

Manual and Fernando, both in black chino pants and white tee shirts and thick, black hair, walked in the front door. Their heads turned toward Ed and Sorrowful, but they walked toward Carlos at the bar.

"Have they paid yet?" asked Manuel.

"No."

"Then let's collect and throw them both out."

"No," said Carlos, his hand raised. "The big one is a well known local personage. Very influential, I would say. Not the kind of people we'd want to alienate."

They turned back to the argument just as Ed's hand shot out and slapped Sorrowful's fat cheek. Sorrowful did not immediately strike back. Instead, his face got red as he stared at Ed in enraged disbelief.

"Now?" asked Fernando.

"Not yet."

Sorrowful took a wide, slow swing at Ed, but Ed easily dodged it and began to laugh. Both men sat still another moment before Sorrowful swung and missed again. He started to struggle out of his seat. Ed jumped out before Sorrowful could get up and swung to slap Sorrowful's face again. But Sorrowful bulled forward. Ed's arm swung harmlessly against the side of Sorrowful's head. They grasped each other by the clothes and tried to push, but Sorrowful was too heavy for Ed to move, and Ed was too wiry for Sorrowful, so neither was able to budge the other.

"Now?" asked Fernando.

The fighters stood grappling in an empty space in the floor where they could do no damage to the furniture. Carlos studied them calmly.

"No. Not yet."

"Which do you think will win?" Manuel asked. "I have five dollars that says the thin one will."

Fernando took another look. The fighters were locked in an inert, red-faced horn-lock. "I have to agree," said Fernando. "The thin gringo will prove himself to be possessed of far superior endurance."

The two young men looked at Carlos, who squinted as he watched. "No, my ten dollars says Senor Jones, the man of used cars, will eventually prevail."

Sorrowful lost his balance when Ed tried to back up, and now they tumbled to the floor, grunting and grasping and scratching. Neither Ed nor Sorrowful looked strong enough to inflict much damage on the other, and the Mexicans began to joke that this was like watching two girls fight in a school yard. But on the floor, where balance was no longer an issue for the two drunken men, Sorrowful finally managed to get on top of Ed, who was unable to move once the full weight of Sorrowful sat on his abdomen. The hammy hands of Sorrowful Jones, the man of used cars, pinned those of Ed, the man of publicities, to the floor and held them there.

"We're doing it my way, goddam it!"

Ed could only grunt, and after several minutes of trying to twist away from the droplets of Sorrowful's sweat that bounced onto his face, Ed ceased even the grunting.

Carlos smiled as he picked up the two five dollar bills on the counter. "Now you may intervene," he said.

Sorrowful felt instant relief when Manual and Fernando pulled him off Ed and helped the equally compliant Ed up from the floor. Ed and Sorrowful collapsed into their booth. Sweat poured from Sorrowful as he sat heaving. He loosened the knot of his necktie, which Ed had pulled almost to the choking point.

Carlos brought a pitcher of ice water and two green plastic tumblers. "Ole, ole," he said. "Do we feel much better now?"

SORROWFUL JONES stood in the middle of the studio floor, a mural-sized photograph of his used car lot projected on the white wall behind him. Sorrowful wore a barrel with shoulder straps. His pudgy bare legs stuck out from the bottom as if they were part of the barrel, whereas the head, shoulders, and arms looked stranded, unattached to anything else. The sweat matted his short, sparse hair against his scalp. With makeup weighting the already sagging flesh of his face, Sorrowful looked like a slow-witted monk.

"Hold it," Ed said. He stepped from behind the camera and put his hands on his hips. "Look, Sorrowful. You're sweating, but you just don't look all that worried. Let's have the *worried* look." Sorrowful knew exactly what Ed was talking about.

"The moron look, you mean?"

"Yeah. The moron look. The basset hound look. The one that you're so damned sure sells cars." Ed stepped back behind the camera.

Sorrowful tried again. He stared at the camera until his gaze sank through it into nowhere. He pulled his jaw back and thrust his head forward. Finally, he contracted the muscles in his nostrils to narrow his nose and pinch his high voice to make it sound alarmed.

Sorrowful had written the script himself. Ed, as usual, started things with an offstage voice.

"Is that you, Sorrowful? Where you been hidin', boy? You look like you lost your last friend."

Sorrowful shook his head slowly. "It's much worse than that, Ed. I done lost my last *Dodge*. They done took all my cars and didn't give me hardly *nothin'* for 'em."

"Yeah, everybody says Sorrowful Jones is a pushover for used car prices."

"I know, Ed. Lord knows I try to stand up for myself." Sorrowful jerked himself up a little straighter and changed his expression to a scowl. "I ain't the pushover some people say I am."

"Well, you're gonna have to be tough this week, Sorrowful, because everybody's gonna be after *this* little number. How about a '66 Plymouth Fury III. Loaded."

"No!" Sorrowful hollered. "It's got a scratch on the gas cap compartment cover. It ain't good enough for my customers! Tell 'em they don't want that one, Ed!"

"And with more horse power than the Hoover Dam," Ed ranted. "Or this sizzling little 1970 Chevy convertible at the outrageous price of only nine hundred dollars!"

"Ed, that one was my grandmother's! I can't sell that!"

"The price? Ha ha ha. Nine hundred bucks. That's what *Sorrowful* says, but everybody knows that Sorrowful Jones is a soft touch. He really does *give* these cars away."

The video had been showing the cars but now it switched back to Sorrowful, whose face was wide-eyed with terror.

"No, not the Chevy! That was Granny's . . ." Sorrowful sensed that the time was right to cry, but he'd never learned how to make real tears come, so he buried his face in the crook of his arm and sobbed. But then the tears began to well, he could feel them, and he pitched his head back to face the camera as he squeezed out what felt like a quart of tears and felt them stream down his face, blending with the sweat that had gathered under the sizzling studio lights. Sorrowful Jones felt his entire being bulge with emotion.

Ed correctly sensed that it was time to zoom in tight on Sorrowful's face and start the banjo music that had for these many years been Sorrowful's theme. Ed just couldn't stop himself from smiling.

"Come on out and see these wonderful values, folks," Ed droned. "And then talk price with *soft* Sorrowful Jones. Ya Hee-ya? Sorrowful Jones Used Cars. 2200 Fifth Avenue."

Sorrowful, his face streaming, broke into a wide, demonic grin. "Sorrowful Jones is *back*!"

Cafe Roma

AFTER FORTY YEARS of working for everyone else in town, Rocks Romano finally had his own place. Cafe Roma was near The Strip, an established restaurant neighborhood where Rocks had tended bar for almost forty years. Cafe Roma was classy by Rocks's standards. The main feature was a vast, polished oak bar that took up an entire wall. Rocks was also very proud of the parquet floors in the dining room and the tinted street-side windows that let the customers see out but did not let those outside see in. Rocks felt that the tinted windows lent the Cafe an air of clubbish exclusivity. And people driving by on slow nights wouldn't be able to see the emptiness inside and assume the place wasn't any good. Rocks had been in the restaurant business too long, he liked to tell everyone, not to know all the negative things people could think. The classiest fact of all was that Rocks had hired a real chef, a guy named Andre, out of New Orleans. Although Rocks initially resisted the idea of a Louisiana-style menu, his youngest son, Louie, convinced him that Birmingham people went to New Orleans all the time and a Cajun menu would be a big hit. Once Rocks became convinced that Cajun was the way to go, he hired Andre sight-unseen, over the phone. When Andre arrived in Birmingham, he turned out to be a slight, secretive man who talked to himself in what Rocks assumed was French, although it was really Bulgarian. Andre was swarthy and hirsute, his lower face darkened by an irrepressible five-o'clock shadow that was in full bloom by noon. He always looked as if he'd just been caught stealing.

Other than Andre and two black helpers in the kitchen, the place was family-run. Rocks had ordered them all to get involved: his four grown kids, his wife, Bobbie, his own parents, and Bobbie's parents. Every one of them had some sort of food business experience. The place was bound to succeed. Except for the fact that Rocks managed to sabotage the whole venture from the very beginning.

First of all, he named it Cafe Roma, since his family name was Romano. People confused Cafe Roma with *Club* Roma, a gay bar three blocks farther north. Cafe Roma was also an odd name for a place with a mostly Cajun menu, and some people who didn't know the place or the family came in expecting Italian food, only to leave as soon as they saw the menu. But much worse than those problems was the fact that fewer and fewer people went downtown at night to eat anymore; they all went to the new chain restaurants at the malls. Nearly every downtown restaurant, even those that had been in business for ten years or longer, was on hard times.

But Rocks had worked out a great deal on the lease with an unsuspecting landlord. Rocks had some inside information that the local newspaper was going to build a new high-rise office building (staffed by three shifts of workers) on the next block. Rocks hurried to close the deal on Cafe Roma just two days before the building project was announced in the paper. The only problem, Rocks discovered as he read the official story, was that construction wouldn't begin for almost a year.

Meanwhile, Rocks had either mortgaged or sold everything he owned, earmarking the proceeds from each sale for a specific item of restaurant equipment. He sold his Oldsmobile for three thousand dollars, bought a battered old Chevy for four hundred, and used the difference to buy a walk-in freezer, two secondhand refrigerators, and four tub sinks at a local restaurant equipment auction. He moved his big-screen TV to the bar and ordered Louie, his youngest son, to move his expensive stereo system to the restaurant as well. Rocks garage-saled most of his clothes to buy sixty-eight white linen tablecloths and almost three hundred napkins. He sold his hunting rifles to buy silverware, his coin collection to buy crystal. And he remortgaged his house to finance the ten-year lease and most of the remodeling. Altogether, it cost just over sixty thousand dollars to open the doors at Cafe Roma.

But that was okay, Rocks told everyone. The place was going to fly. It would be the hottest restaurant in Birmingham before the year was out, and once the newspaper opened its new office building, the Cafe would be open around the clock. They had plenty of parking, a unique menu, and a well known owner. Rocks figured he'd mixed a drink for everyone over twenty-one within a fifty-mile radius of Birmingham.

But that was another part of Cafe Roma's recipe for uncertainty; Rocks was a bartender who had never managed anything. So Rocks appointed Louie, who had managed a hotdog joint for a year, to be general manager of Cafe Roma. This created bad feelings among Rocks's other three kids, who felt that Louie, even at thirty, was too young to be manager. Rocks quickly discovered that the only way to get everyone to work in the place was to make each one manager of something. So Gina, the oldest, who had worked one summer as a hostess, became dining room manager. Joey, who sometimes drove a truck for a beer distributor, was named beverage manager, and Rudolfo, a short-order cook at a local pancake restaurant, was made kitchen manager.

Bobbie, who wanted as little as possible to do with the place, went through the motions of being the hostess.

They were an unlikely staff for what Rocks had hoped would be a classy restaurant. For one thing, they were not very attractive people. Rocks looked like an ex-con, with a dwindling number of white hairs cut in a flattop, a scar on his cheek from a car accident thirty years ago, and a buzzard neck that made his face jut out a foot beyond his chest. His Adam's apple looked like an unswallowed golf ball. In his too-large suit, he looked as if he had lost twenty pounds that very day.

Bobbie was much bigger than Rocks, and her balloonish, made-up face looked as if it might burst at any moment. In her normal mode, she held stock-still and stared off into space, so when she made even the smallest movement, it was as if she had startled herself.

Gina was a thin, ravaged woman who could not utter a sentence, even a one-word sentence, without using profanity. Her straight hair had been bleached so many times it was four different shades of yellow-white, depending on how close to her scalp you looked. Her teeth were ragged, with large gaps between those that remained. Her makeup—Rocks called it her war paint—made her look utterly ferocious.

Joey, who had twice done time for assault with a deadly weapon, was trying to go straight. As long as he took his tranquilizers, he remained calm and vacuously cooperative. But Joey had a notoriously poor memory. He was rail thin everywhere but in his belly, which hung over his belt like a flour sack. His face was gaunt, with large shadows around his eyes, and his eyebrows had gone completely gray.

Rudy was the only truly fat child of Rocks and Bobbie, a clone of his mother. He weighed over two hundred when he was thirteen; now, at thirty-six and five foot eight, he hovered near three hundred, depending on how badly he had binged in the kitchen that day. He was red-faced, sluggish, usually grinning except when he was angry. Then he stormed and bellowed and threw things, and when he finally calmed down, he ate for several hours to soothe his jangled nerves.

The grandparents weren't much help. The two families had never been particularly friendly, since Bobbie's people were from Sicily and Rocks's were from Naples. At the Cafe, they occupied two tables at opposite corners of the restaurant, creating the aura of impending war as they sat all day scrutinizing and criticizing everything that went on. If any of them actually bussed a few dishes or carried water to a table, they complained about it until they went home.

Of the entire Romano-Lapomada clan, only Louie seemed normal. He was small-shouldered and thin, clean-cut, friendly, yet aloof and thoughtful as he worked. Louie was a detail man who could not only picture in his mind how things needed to be, he could also make them that way—from the Cafe Roma logo on the matchbooks to the exact amount of crawfish to keep in stock. He had grown up with an ability to see the dark side of things and anticipate whatever could go wrong. For this reason, he was appalled that Rocks had not budgeted money for insurance. At the very least they needed liability insurance, Louie argued. And they needed fire and theft insurance. But Rocks insisted that equipment and supplies were the most important things right now. They could buy insurance after the place was making some money.

"But what if somebody stumbles on the way out the door, falls down on the sidewalk, breaks a knee and sues us?"

"Naw. Most of the folks coming in here ain't going to sue us. They're friends. Friends don't sue you."

Louie knew better. Even your friends sued you because they didn't think of it as suing *you*, they thought of it as suing your insurance company.

"That's what I mean," Rocks said. "If they thought we had insurance, they might sue. But as long as they know we don't, ain't nobody gonna sue us."

"Right. And what if somebody tries to rob us?"

Rocks led Louie around behind the bar and showed him the pistol hidden under a stack of counter towels. "Loaded," Rocks said. "The cheapest, best robbery insurance there is."

LIKE EVERYONE else in the Romano family, Louie was quick-tempered, but his temper ebbed as quickly as it flared. It usually flared for good reason; no one in the restaurant knew what to do, and they refused to learn from Louie because he was the youngest. So Louie quietly went about trying to do everything himself. If Gina terrorized a waitress, Louie gave the sobbing girl ten dollars and a shot of Jack Daniels. If he found Rudy abusing the dishwasher, he gave the dishwasher the rest of the night off and washed the dishes himself. And if Joey had forgotten to take his medication and got too nervous and insulting to deal with the customers, Louie sent Joey home and Rocks tended bar.

Rocks never minded tending bar. He had not appointed himself manager of anything. Instead, Rocks assigned himself to pacing around the restaurant, shrinking ever further into his wrinkled suit as he glared at the customers for not eating and drinking more. Being nice to the customers was not his job, he had decided; his job was to be the owner. His two primary responsibilities were to worry a lot and to second-guess all of Louie's decisions.

So it was Louie who went to the tables to say hello to customers and ask them if they liked their food. It was Louie who intervened in the kitchen whenever Rudy tried to give orders to Andre, the paranoid chef from Bulgaria via New Orleans. Louie had privately told Andre to ignore Rudy and to do things any way he wanted. As long as the food was good and it got to the tables in a reasonable amount of time, Louie didn't care if Andre worked naked, drunk, stoned, or a combination of the three. Louie, of course, was the one who intercepted the small groups of gays who, by chance, came chattering and laughing into the Cafe and sent them down the street to *Club* Roma before any of the straight customers got nervous. "But this place looks nice. I *love* etouffee food. That's what I call *anything* made in New Orleans. And I love that Cajun music you're playing." "All out of etouffee food tonight, boys," Louie would say as he herded them toward the door. "All we've got is hamburgers. There's a really good place just down the street. I think it's called Club Roma. I believe that's the place you're trying to find."

"Oh, we thought *this* . . . "

"Have a nice night."

And it was Louie who insisted on doing the hiring for Cafe Roma, since, as he put it to Rocks, Gina and Rudy couldn't tell a waitress or a dishwasher from a light bulb. Louie had worked in a few of the better restaurants in town. He knew restaurant talent when he saw it, and he saw it in Alicia when she came in to apply for a job.

Alicia was a dark-skinned young black woman with the slender nose, thin lips, and demure manner of a princess. Along with her beige suit she wore silver pendant earrings, a silver necklace, silver bracelets, and silver rings on her long fingers. She had a sleepy, flirtatious smile in her eyes that sent Louie into a quiet fit. He guessed she was about twenty-five. She was short, like him, and just as thin. She spoke standard English that was better than Louie's. They sat at a corner table, away from the parents and grandparents, as Louie interviewed her. Alicia was animated, her hands in constant and languid motion as she laughed and talked with Louie, flashing him sideways smiles and giving coy replies to his questions, some of which were personal. Married? Not anymore. Seeing anyone? No, there wasn't anybody she knew who came up to her standards.

"Louie!" Rocks called from the kitchen door.

"Excuse me a moment," Louie said as he stood up. He was pretty sure he knew what Rocks had on his mind.

"Why are you bothering to interview her? We don't want no nigger waitresses," Rocks whispered harshly. "Back out in the kitchen, that's one thing. I don't want no niggers out front."

"What if she's a good waitress?"

"I don't care if she'd be a good president."

"Tough shit, Daddy. I already hired her."

Rocks paled. "You what?"

"I hired her. If I go back and un-hire her, she'll sue us for discrimination. And I'll personally help her find a lawyer."

Louie strode back to the table where Alicia waited. Something in the way she locked onto his eyes told him she knew he had just stood up for her. And had won.

"When can you start?"

"When do you want me?" she asked, shifting herself a little and recrossing her legs.

ROCKS STOPPED complaining about Alicia after her first few nights on the job. Louie assumed that everyone had gotten used to her. Based on the tips he saw on her tables, Louie surmised that the customers liked her, too. He tried not to notice her long, alluring looks or the moments when she brushed against him as they passed each other in the kitchen, or as Louie helped her set up tables. But Louie found himself thinking about her almost constantly. During the hour before she arrived at work each day, he looked at his watch every minute, and when she finally walked in the door, his knees began to tremble and his breath rasped in his throat like a sandy wind in the trees. On her night off, Monday, Louie had to drag himself to work. He tried to imagine what she was like away from the restaurant, but he had no factual fuel for his imaginings. She had told him at her interview that she was a student, but he had not asked her where she went to school. All Louie knew about her was her name, Alicia Hargrove, and her phone number, which he had committed to memory rather than write it down somewhere and lose it.

Louie didn't want to appear too friendly or chatty toward her or to acknowledge her minor flirtations, since that could resurrect Rocks's objections to her presence at the Cafe. It was impossible to talk to her out of earshot of a sibling or grandparent, so Louie limited his conversation to the most superficial, work-related niceties. How are you tonight? Your tables are all set up. You're welcome. Yes, I heard about the concert; we may get a few extra customers. You never know what to expect in this business. He longed to tell her that her necklaces and her silk blouses made his hands itch to touch her; or that he had been awake all night, naked and simmering as he thought about her. But he said nothing. He told himself to concentrate only on the restaurant. Too much depended on him these days.

For the first two months that the cafe was open business was good because Rocks really did know everybody in town, and they all felt obligated to come by the Cafe at least once to say hello and let Rocks know they had been there. Hardly any of them came back. The food was weird, Louie had overheard a few people saying. Who wanted to eat rabbit spaghetti and *boo dan*, whatever the hell that was? Rocks's friends were mostly steak and potatoes people who ate ketchup on their fried eggs and pot roast. They preferred hamburger buns to the fresh French bread that Andre baked everyday. They all made an appearance. At least one. But even when the cafe was crowded it lacked the laughter and bustle of the truly successful restaurants that Louie and Rocks had observed over the years. The customers came, but they didn't seem to have much fun. They ate silently and grimly as the Cajun singers yowled on the stereo above the polite clinking of Rocks's expensive silverware. Louie noticed that they left a lot on their plates.

"How was it?" Rocks would challenge them as he collected their money. "Everything okay?"

"Great. Just great. Different. Good luck, Rocks. It was great to see you again."

"Come back, now."

"We will."

But they didn't. Within a few weeks of the big opening, revenues dropped from about fourteen hundred dollars a night to six hundred. Rocks, shrinking ever further into his only suit, either paced or stood by the large windows that looked out onto the street. Behind him, two waitresses, a chef, a dishwasher, two kitchen helpers and a bunch of relatives spent most of their time sitting around, either watching TV or sleeping. Rocks only allowed the stereo to be played when customers came in. He hated Louie's selection of music and much preferred the droning announcers of ESPN to Cajun fiddles and accordions. Had it not been for the two booths of employees and the three tables of family, Cafe Roma would have looked deserted.

Rocks was sure he knew what was wrong; it was that black waitress. No one he knew wanted to come into a place where there was a black working out front. If there was one, sooner or later there'd be a tribe of them. Word would get out. It probably already had.

Rocks watched Alicia for a moment as she wiped down the seats in the booths. Then he went into the kitchen looking for Louie. He found him in the walk-in, inventorying the bags of frozen shrimp and crawfish.

"Louie," he said. "I want you to fire the staff until we got more business. Get rid of two or three in the kitchen. And those waitresses."

"What brought *this* on?"

"I ain't having a bunch of lard-asses sit around and watch TV on my dime."

"What are they supposed to do if there's no business?"

"Go home."

"Okay, Daddy. How's this? I'll cut everybody's hours, but I don't want to let anyone go. If we need them later, I don't want any bad feelings."

"Just make sure you fire Lizette and Alicia."

"Alicia's our best worker."

"I don't care. You know how I feel about that."

"Forget it, Daddy. I'll cut everyone's hours, but I'm the one who's going to decide who gets cut how much."

Rocks went back to the dining room. The last customers had left, and Rocks surveyed a dining room full of well-fed goldbrickers whose eyes were glued to the TV screen. Except Alicia, who always made herself look busy.

Rocks turned off the TV. "Let's get some work done around here," he ordered. "Mop that floor! Polish the bar!"

The help slowly climbed out of the booths, their faces dark and annoyed at being interrupted.

Rocks noticed Alicia across the way watching him as she wiped down the front window, smiling her curious, perpetual smile. She was always smiling, damn her, Rocks thought. But he knew it was an act; underneath the smile, she was just as resentful and impudent as the others. He'd bet money on it, if he ever had to.

II

Under the reorganization of Cafe Roma, Rocks was the opener and Louie the closer. Rocks came in at nine in the morning and went home around six at night. Gina, Joey, and Rudy found other jobs, and Bobbie and the in-laws stopped spending their days at the cafe. Bobbie eventually took a part-time job as a mail room clerk at an insurance company. Rocks also laid off Andre, who threatened to sue them for bringing him to Birmingham and then letting him go after only three months. Andre and his high salary were a welcome absence.

Wayne, who had worked as Andre's assistant since Cafe Roma opened and had learned all his recipes, became chef, although the promotion did not include a raise. Nonetheless, it was a big step up for Wayne, who had never been anything but a fry cook and chef's assistant. Wayne was a rotund, good-natured black man of about thirty-five. He and Louie had worked together at two other restaurants, and they had become semi-friends. Wayne worked hard when there were customers, and sipped beer and dozed in the kitchen, snoring and talking in his sleep when there were none.

The slimmed-down staff left only Wayne and Alicia, who was informed by Rocks when Louie wasn't there that if she wanted to stay on, it would be for tips only.

When Louie returned from spending his last cash on fifty pounds of ground beef and learned that Rocks had made Alicia an offer she had to refuse, he was livid.

"I didn't *fire* her. Besides, what's it to you, son? She's just hired help."

"She was a damned good worker."

"She can be a good worker somewhere else."

"Goddam it, Daddy . . . " He made an excuse to go back out—to buy a rack and a few bags of pretzels and popcorn for the bar. He found a phone booth and called the number he had memorized. After ten rings, a husky, sleepy male voice answered.

"May I speak to Alicia?"

"Who?"

"Alicia."

"They ain't no Alicia stay here."

"Alicia Hargrove?"

The line went dead after a few seconds, and Louie made himself acknowledge the fact that Alicia was not her real name. He knew that black girls might give a guy they met in a bar a phony telephone number, but this number was supposed to be for real, since she'd given it to her employer. He stood in the phone booth a moment, wondering if he wasn't acting a bit foolish. He decided he was and drove back to the cafe.

Louie stopped thinking about Alicia during the day and started looking at other women for a change. But look was all he did. And he still thought about Alicia most nights.

Cafe Roma was now a quiet, lifeless place. Wayne came in when Rocks did, cooked for all ten lunch customers, then went home from about one until five. Louie came in at five-thirty, just before Rocks left. The Cajun menu was dropped, except for the red beans and rice, and now the cafe served mainly burgers, omelets, and Cajun hot sausage sandwiches, since Louie had bought a huge stock of Cajun sausage at an irresistible discount when they opened the cafe.

Business was slim and grim.

When Wayne wasn't napping, he and Louie shot pool on the table Louie had moved from home into a storage room that he and Rocks had hoped one day to turn into a game room. Louie was never a great pool player, and Wayne regularly took a few dollars off him. Between what he won from Louie and his salary for doing damned little, Wayne was making out just fine, Louie often reflected. But it would be over a year before the new newspaper building would be open, and something had to happen before then if the cafe was going to last that long. Louie knew it was up to him to save the place, if it was savable.

He knew the local night scene. He knew that no one was open late except the all-night breakfast chains, and that there might be a market there for the cafe to tap. Louie started staying open all night to serve breakfast to the stragglers—the musicians, cabbies, cops, an occasional bum who had scraped up some change. He stopped turning away the gays who came there by accident—and then came back night after night because they liked the relative emptiness of the place, and the fact that they could feel comfortable there after their own places turned the lights off. Louie played disco music on the stereo and let them dance, if that was what they wanted to do. The windows were tinted, no one could see inside. So what if the cabbies and cops stopped coming? The new clientele grew by the week as word got out. Louie started staying open until six in the morning.

He didn't mind the hours; he'd spent the better part of two years working the all-night shift at a Waffle House, a place where lots of gays had always hung out. Louie had never told Rocks that he actually knew a few gays well enough to speak to them on the street.

Although they seldom took in more than six or seven hundred dollars a night, business was too hectic for just Louie and Wayne to handle. Louie decided to try Alicia's phone number once more, and this time it was she who answered. The sound of her voice made his knees quiver.

"This is Louie."

She seemed hesitant at first. "Louie . . . hi!"

"Alicia isn't your real name, is it?"

"I have different names for different purposes," she said, no apology in her voice.

"What name would you use if I asked you to come back to work?"

"What name would you want to give me?"

"All-night Alicia."

She laughed. "Is that the name or the hours?"

"Both."

"When do I start?"

"How about eleven tonight?"

She hesitated a moment. "I've kind of missed you . . . . Is it all right if I come a little earlier than that?"

THE EARLY EVENING was still a quiet time at the cafe, and Louie was sitting at the bar drinking a mai tai, his specialty, when Alicia arrived at seven. Her soft eyes gripped him from the moment she walked in. She seemed even more familiar with him than when he used to see her everyday. She wore designer jeans, high heels, her usual silk blouse—this one royal blue—and feathery earrings. She sat down, lay her purse on the bar, and leaned toward him to kiss his cheek. His skin went taut at the cool touch of her lips.

"Hi there," she said.

Louie could no longer contain his trembling, and he clamped his hands between his knees. "Hi there yourself."

"What are you drinking?"

"Mai tai. Want one?"

"No. Not just yet. How about a Coke?"

They sat at the bar and talked like old friends. Louie reminded himself that this was the first time they'd ever been alone together, and he could not imagine that he had lived almost three months without seeing her.

She was, she now admitted, married. Reginald was a jazz guitarist and a crack dealer, who slept around all over Birmingham. Alicia claimed that she wanted to divorce him but didn't have the money to move into her own place.

Louie, who had never been a fighter, ached to kill the bastard. The infidelity Louie didn't mind; that would make it okay for Alicia to sleep with Louie, if it ever came to that. But the stories of beatings and insults were torturous to Louie. He mourned the loss of the ten thousand dollars he had withdrawn from his savings and sunk into the cafe. If he only had it now. A little after nine, Alicia let Louie make her a mai tai. He'd already had three. They touched each other's arms and hands and thighs as they talked and laughed together. After her second mai tai, Alicia leaned to kiss him again, only this time their mouths touched. It was a long, earnest and yet tender kiss, a game of tongue tag that stopped short of outright invasion. Louie's mind wandered far away from the cafe as her ear came to rest against his shoulder and their lips stayed together.

The door opened. "Knock knock. Caught ya!"

It was Rheingold, the architect from Chicago. Three of his friends trooped in behind him.

"Turn up that *music*. I *love* the big band sound."

Louie squeezed her hand and got down from his bar stool, his head ringing, his eyes moist. "Later," he whispered.

"I hope so."

The night lurched along interminably. Louie drank in her eyes as they flashed at him across the bar or across the room. They touched briefly whenever possible, too busy with each other to think anyone noticed. But all of Rheingold's friends seemed to catch the message in the air.

The tall, dark-haired one who called himself Ziegfeld Folly breathed loudly and fanned himself with his fedora hat as he looked at Alicia. "It's so *warm* in here."

"My *god*," Rheingold told Alicia, "let us finish these drinks and leave so you people can get down to business!"

As soon as they were gone, Louie locked the door, cut the lights, and sent Wayne home. With his last one hundred dollars, Louie got them a few hours in the new Hyatt Hotel downtown. In the dim light from the street lamps far below, they came to know every inch of each other. When they touched, their fingers or hair or breath lay upon the other with the perfect weight, and when they spoke, they finished each other's sentences. It was like that all night. They never slept for more than thirty minutes at a time before they awoke to make love again.

EACH NIGHT before the rush of customers started, Louie and Alicia made love in one of the storage closets or restrooms (the ladies' room was carpeted), or on Louie's pool table in the back room. After a week, Louie bought a small mattress and some cheap linen. A week later he bought expensive linen.

Meanwhile, Wayne cooked, tended bar, waited on tables and washed the dishes by himself. Louie knew Wayne helped himself to the good Scotch and imported beer, but he got the job done, and he covered for Louie while he and Alicia lay together in the lightless pool room, a fan blowing the dark air in a hard whisper over their sweating bodies as the stereo shook the walls with its monotonous disco beat.

Around midnight, Louie and Alicia would get dressed and emerge into the glare of the dimly lit dining room. The regular customers applauded, often with a standing ovation, whenever Louie and Alicia emerged from the pool room.

"God save the king!" Rheingold liked to shout.

"The queens, too," Louie shouted back. The place roared and squealed, and Louie turned the stereo up even louder and laughed as the boys danced. Louie and Wayne started to become good enough friends to joke with each other. Wayne called Louie White Boss, and Louie called Wayne Darkie. They called Alicia Sabu, the Jungle Princess. "Darkie, scrub down the straws of this broom for me, please," Louie might say as the three of them played gin rummy at the bar. "And cut some up in little pieces. We're out of toothpicks."

"Yassuh, White Boss."

"Y'all ain't got enough to do around here," Sabu would say, slipping into jive whenever she was around Wayne. Louie was aware of the way Wayne's eyes made their way all over Alicia, but Louie had grown up around black kids and knew exactly how black men looked at women. Louie didn't take it to mean anything.

When the customers allowed Louie to choose the music, the stereo blasted B.B. King and Muddy Water and Robert Johnson tapes that Louie had brought from home. "My *grandfather* used to listen this stuff," Sabu said scornfully. "You too *young* to be listening to this old nigger

music." Louie hated to hear her talk that way, especially to hear her call
her people niggers. But that, too, he knew to be their way. She was at least
two people, he had concluded: a refined, mannerly, almost regal one, and
a raw, trash-talking ghetto kid who had seen far more of life than Louie
had. He wanted her to have only her soft side, the one that could be kind
to people, even after she had accurately assessed their flaws, a skill that
Louie found very amusing in her. Except when her parodies of people hit
a little too close to home. For instance, when she did her version of
Rocks. She could stick out her neck at exactly the right angle and
summon the perfect rasp in her voice. "Clean them got-dam windas.
Wipe this here. Mop that there." She had Rocks's way of not just
pointing but jabbing. Her act put Wayne into a head-wrenching fit.
Louie laughed too, but uneasily. It was one thing for *him* to criticize
Rocks, but seeing someone outside his family do it made Louie sad, and
he disliked himself for laughing along with Wayne. When they were
alone in the dark, Sabu became Alicia again and spoke correct English in
reedy whispers against his ear. Then Louie's uneasiness evaporated. She
was very much the lady she appeared to be, he told himself.

She had begun to tell him about herself, and the shedding of her
secrecy further assured Louie that she was everything he wanted her to be.
She had an associate degree in cosmetology but had decided she didn't
want to spend her life making the kinky hair of black women straight and
perming the straight hair of white women into curls. It didn't make
sense. Now she was in her last semester of work toward a bachelor's
degree in biology, with a dual major in theater. That explained her
uncanny ability to parody Rocks, Louie saw now. Had she considered a
career as an actress, he asked her. No. Acting was fun, but it was too
unstable to make it a career. Instead, she was thinking about going to
medical school.

She had come a long way. She had seven brothers and sisters, all of
them older, but she was the first one in her family to go to college. It was
one of her teachers, Miss Travis, who had turned her around. Miss Travis
was the only white teacher in Alicia's all-black high school. Miss Travis
was always taking the kids on field trips to the zoo and the botanical

gardens. One time, she had the children write essays for a contest called "I have a dream," which was to celebrate Martin Luther King Day.

"The class won a trip to the Coca-Cola headquarters in Atlanta," Alicia recounted. "The school claimed it didn't have enough money to charter a bus, so Miss Travis chartered the bus with her own money. And she wasn't any rich woman. So we all rode the bus over to Atlanta, and the Coca-Cola people had all this food there waiting for us and some of the kids didn't hardly get to eat much at home, and when they saw all these sandwiches and ice cream and Coca-Colas, they just ate and ate until half of them got sick and had to go back out and lay down in the bus and miss the tour of the Coca-Cola world headquarters.

"And when we got back home to Birmingham about ten o'clock at night, my brother was supposed to come to the school and pick me up. Miss Travis didn't want me waiting all by myself at night, so she stayed with me and we talked and talked. I mean, we talked about everything there was to talk about. She told me I could do anything I wanted to and hoped I wouldn't be just—what was it she said—she hoped I wouldn't end up just another project pregnancy statistic.

"Well, my brother never showed up, and Miss Travis drove me home, right into this mean-ass neighborhood that even scared most of the black folk who lived there. I never in my whole life ever saw white people come there, except white cops. She brought me home and even saw me to the door and told my mother it was a shame nobody ever came to pick me up.

"Then she left to go home, but she got lost and a couple of young gang guys shot up her car and hit her in the shoulder. I felt real bad when I went to see her in the hospital, but she told me not to worry about it, she'd do the same thing the next night if I needed a ride home. But she made me promise right then and there that I'd stay in school and try to make something of myself. So that's what I'm going to do."

The story made Louie's eyes red. Alicia laughed.

"Don't cry for me, White Boy. I'm on the way up!"

Louie had tried one semester of college and dropped out. He liked the idea that the woman he loved was well educated, whether he was or

not. And she was ambitious. Louie told himself it was time to make some
real money out of the cafe so that he could help this intelligent, aspiring
young woman to be the fine physician he knew she would be if only she
got the chance.

LIKE HIS FATHER, Louie knew a lot of people in the restaurant
business. So he started stopping by the other restaurants on Southside in
the evening, renewing old acquaintances with bartenders and waiters and
cooks and letting them know that Cafe Roma was the new late-night
scene for people like them, a place to come and be waited on when they
were finished waiting on everybody else. Alicia, who had also worked in
Southside restaurants, began bringing in some of her friends, too, and in
a few weeks, Cafe Roma was taking in a little over a thousand dollars a
night just on Louie's shift. It was a mixed crowd, indeed; whites, blacks,
lesbians and gays, mostly restaurant people and musicians, but a whole
lot of people Louie didn't know, too. It dazzled him to see so many
people there, almost as many as when he and Rocks first opened and all
the Italians in town came. And they all fit in together. The cafe, Louie
sometimes reflected, had more the feeling of somebody's den than a
restaurant. It was loud with music and laughter but never rowdy. When
people got drunk they got friendly drunk, never mean; and they drove
each other home rather than let anyone drive drunk.

Louie often wondered how the same people could come in night
after night and stay for hours, but he was glad they did. He had pocket
money once again and was re-feathering his once respectable savings
account. Alicia's customers were more than just customers, they were
worshippers. Louie told himself he was happy for her to have so many
admirers. She was good for business, and she was the best thing that had
ever happened to him. With the cafe's new prosperity, Louie and Alicia
had less time to spend together. They started meeting one or two
afternoons a week at a motel on Southside. When they weren't making
love, they were plotting Alicia's divorce and how they would get married
the moment the ink on the divorce decree was dry.

"Your father's going to really love this," Alicia always laughed whenever she and Louie talked about marriage.

"We'll just tell him you're from the branch of the family that fled to Africa when Caesar took over."

"Has your Daddy ever in his life laughed?"

Louie smiled. "Yeah. Once. I remember it well. But it turned out he just had a little gas."

Their favorite thing to talk about was life without other people in the world. They would move to a remote Caribbean island, or a farm in Nova Scotia and raise their own food, put on clothes only in bad weather, start a mail-order business of some kind so that they could make a lot of money but never leave the ten or twenty acres of sanity they would carve for themselves.

"Is this for real, Louie? Do you really love me, or is it just the novelty of sleeping with a black girl? Tell me honestly."

"Baby, I'd love you if you were purple."

"And will you help me with that charge account at Rich's I was telling you about last night?"

"Of course."

"I had to buy all those clothes for interviews when I was looking for a job."

"I know. You don't have to explain."

She smiled for a moment, then her face looked troubled. "Could I ask you for another favor?"

"Sure."

"I wish you wouldn't act so jealous and ugly when I go somewhere with my friends for breakfast after we close up."

"But don't you feel like you should help me close up?"

"Wayne can help you, baby. I get so tired by the time six o'clock rolls around . . . "

"Yeah. You're so tired you just have to take off with your friends."

She looked hard at him. "Okay. Don't try to change. Just go ahead and be pissy whenever you feel like it."

THEY DIDN'T meet at the motel at all one week. Then she needed money to see the doctor; she had some kind of infection. She wasn't sure what it was exactly, and she didn't have any health insurance, since no one who worked at Cafe Roma had health insurance. Louie didn't ask her what she was doing with all the money she made at the cafe—at least a hundred dollars a night, by his reckoning. He just gave her whatever money she asked for whenever she asked. Most of the time when they were alone together at the cafe, Alicia was quiet. To Louie, her silence was worse than a wall; it was a mine field of wrong things for him to say.

"I'd do anything for you, baby."

"Are you sure?"

He stroked her black, glistening hair, letting his fingers get caught in the curls. "Of course."

"Would you do something bad to Reginald if I needed you to? Like really bad?"

Louie swallowed hard, thinking about her teacher, Miss Travis. "Yes," he said. "If you asked me to. If you really did need me to."

When he was by himself, Louie knew that he was in over his head with Alicia. He felt overmatched. She had so many problems, whereas he had only one.

BOBBIE HAD always been the cafe's bookkeeper, and now the amount of money coming in caught Bobbie's and Rocks's attention. Rocks grew suspicious and drove by the place late one night to see exactly what was going on. After a few days of surveillance, he stayed past his own shift one night to talk to Louie. Louie was stocking the beer cooler and Rocks stood with his hands spread out on the bar. He spoke in a quiet, calm voice.

"Is it true that you're letting queers and niggers in here at night?"

"I'm letting *customers* in, Daddy."

"You're turning this place into a damned joint."

"I'm making money for us. If you don't like the color or the sex of that money, all I can say is too bad."

"Alicia's back."

"That's right. And she brought a lot of new customers with her."

"Are you fucking that little black bitch?"

"It's none of your business, Daddy."

"I thought so." Rocks poked his finger in Louie's chest. "I want you to fire her when she comes in tonight. I knew she was trouble the minute I laid eyes on her. Bringing niggers and queers in here."

"Fuck off, Daddy. It's none of your business. You try to fire her and I walk, too."

It was a standoff, and it created the worst strain Rocks and Louie had ever known. Louie was Rocks's favorite among his kids. Louie, he had always thought, had potential. Rocks had long ago given up wondering where he messed up with the others, but Louie was different—smart, hard-working. He knew how to save a dollar, too; he still lived at home and had his own apartment in the basement. He'd been able to kick in his savings when Rocks bought the cafe.

It was a shame Louie had no sense when it came to women.

That night Rocks stayed at the cafe until one, just so he could see for himself what went on there at night. All his worst suspicions were confirmed. The fags didn't just come in to eat, they pranced around like they owned the place, strutting and dancing with each other, squealing like little girls, and joking with Louie like they'd known him for years and he was one of them. The stereo was so loud it gave Rocks a headache. Niggers everywhere. Rocks didn't care that most of Louie's black customers waited tables in the good restaurants, and that some of them still wore their tuxedos from work. Rocks didn't care how they dressed; this was not his idea of a classy crowd.

And here was his best son, Louie, running his ass off playing step and fetch for them.

"Hey, Daddy, you mind taking cash?" Louie nodded at the small line of people forming at the end of the bar.

"This ain't my shift."

Louie glared. Rocks glared back.

It especially galled Rocks to watch Alicia kiss up to the crowd, literally. The fags had their hands all over her and so did some of the niggers, especially the fag niggers. Rocks had never before heard of a gay black. Sitting in his own restaurant, he had the feeling that he was having a very bad dream.

When things died down a little, Rocks caught up with Louie in the walk-in. "You fire her ass or I'll *let* you walk. This is a disgrace."

"This place wouldn't last a week without me," Louie said. "I walk and my ten grand walks with me. As if you could come up with it."

"That's what you think, you little prick. You can take your piss-ant ten grand any time you like."

"Don't push me, Daddy. I might take you up on that."

"I hope the hell you do. You've *ruined* this place."

III

The next day, Rocks went to visit Steve Wells, a local bookie with whom Rocks had been placing his football bets for many years. After a night of wondering what went wrong, Rocks concluded that the only way to restore the cafe to respectability was to get Louie out; and the only way to do that was to buy him out. Steve Wells was the only guy Rocks knew who had that kind of ready cash. Steve not only had cash to put into the place, he also had lots of friends. If Steve couldn't get regular white people in the cafe at night, nobody could.

Steve was a big, tanned man about Louie's age who had his hair permed and lightened monthly. Now it was beach blond. He divided his time between his condo at Orange Beach and a small office in the high-rise AmSouth building, where the sign on his door said he was a management consultant. He wore expensive suits and shoes in his office. Rocks didn't know how to act around a bookie who dressed like a stock broker.

Steve laughed when Rocks told his story. "Shit, Bubba. Why would I want into a restaurant? That sounds like *work*. My doctor says I'm allergic to work."

"The place could make good money," Rocks said. "With the right people in it."

Steve held his hands out to his sides. "I got money. I believe I'd feel greedy if I had any more."

"I'll let you in cheap. You can give your profits to some charity."

Steve howled over that. "Look, Bubba. What is it you *really* want. Maybe I could help you if you told me what's really on your mind. I believe you ain't telling me the whole story."

So Rocks told Steve what was going on at the cafe. Steve laughed every few words as he pretended to be powerless to run off the riffraff. "Me? Ha Ha. Bubba, I *depend* on riffraff. I *attract* riffraff. All antennas full signal. Ha ha. Kind of like a bitch in heat attracts horny fleas. Ha Ha. So how's Bobbie? How are your folks? They must be old enough to die by now, ain't they?"

"They old all right. But Eye-talians don't die so easy as white folks." Rocks laughed. "I wish to hell you'd help me, Brother."

"I ain't got no beef with riffraff. But I'll tell you something, Rocks. I just feel like I gotta do *some*thing for a guy that's drummed up so much business for me over the years we knowed each other. Ha ha. Put 'er here, Partner."

Rocks thought he would savor the shock and indignation on Louie's face when Rocks broke him the news a few days later. But it only made him sad. Louie had just arrived for work when Rocks told him.

"You what? Without even talking to me about it first? Steve Wells is one of the lowest son-a-bitches in Birmingham. That bastard's belly's never been off the ground."

"You can call him a snake if you want to, son, but you better start calling him partner, too."

Louie tried to sound reasonable, non-confrontational. "Daddy, you're making a mistake."

"What do you care? All you're interested in is—"

"That's not your business, Daddy. The cafe is your business. And my business. It's not Steve Wells's business. He'll be trying to tell you what to do as soon as he's got a damned dime in that door."

"Good," Rocks said. "I hope the hell someone's finally willing to take this bull by the horn. I was sort of hoping you'd be the one to tell me how to make this place work, but you're too busy screwing that—"

Louie had to fight back the indignation. "Daddy, I stay open all night to take in enough to keep the place going."

"Well, we'll knock that all-night shit off when Steve gets in. You can pull out anytime you want. Steve wants us to start advertising big-time. We'll have a decent dinner business again. I never meant to have my restaurant turned into a joint."

"Oh? And having Steve bringing all his gambling pals in here is going to improve things?"

"It'll make it look full in the evening. I kind of like that idea myself."

"It's full now."

"I mean with white people. And *normal* people. I mean full of the kind of people I'd invite home."

"Right, Daddy." Louie started toward the kitchen. "But there's full, and there's full of shit."

Rocks followed Louie into the kitchen. "If you want to hold onto your title of general manager, you need to start spending more time here during the day. Instead of wasting your money on motel rooms. Probably catching all kinds of diseases. I hope to hell you're using a Trojan."

My own father, Louie thought. Spying on me.

THE BAD BLOOD between Louie and Steve went back many years. Louie was a freshman in high school the year Steve was a senior. Steve was one of those big guys who loved to elbow the smaller ones, and Louie was one of the smaller ones Steve had elbowed. Steve had humiliated Louie one time by pushing him down a flight of stairs in front of a girl Louie was going with at the time. Another time, in the boys' room, Steve grabbed Louie's books out of his arms and threw them into an unflushed toilet.

And here was Steve sitting at the bar in an expensive leather jacket, his shirt open almost to his navel. Steve wore a showy gold chain around his neck and a showy gold watch on his wrist. He had bulked up a lot since Louie had last seen him a couple of years earlier. Louie ignored him as long as he could, stacking paper napkins and setting up the bar until Rocks forced him to acknowledge Steve's presence.

"You know Louie, don't you?" Rocks asked, his arm around Steve's shoulder.

Steve shook his head. "Can't say as I do. Hi, Louie."

In view of how well Louie remembered Steve, the fact that Steve did not remember him made Louie both furious and relieved. Louie turned away from Steve's extended hand and went back to the kitchen, where he began to berate the new dishwasher Rocks had hired that day without consulting Louie on his decision.

"Dwight, what the hell are you doing reading a magazine? Get this goddam kitchen floor mopped!"

"It ain't dirty."

"Then get your ass out the door! I'll find a dishwasher who wants to work!"

Rocks came into the kitchen a moment later. "Who the hell do you think you are, snubbing Steve like that?"

"He's a shit."

"You sorry little . . . Didn't anybody ever tell you that you don't bite the damned hand that's feeding you?"

"That son of a bitch isn't feeding me, Daddy. He's feeding you. Through his ass."

"I'm just trying to make this thing work. I've waited too long to have my own place."

"And now you're going to junk it up with a turd like Steve and his sleazy friends?"

Rocks winced and dropped his voice to a near-whisper. "Keep your voice down. He can probably hear you."

"Good." Louie turned back to the dishwasher, who continued to sit on the dish chute reading his magazine. "I said for you to mop that floor." Louie was on the verge of hysteria. He could feel his pulse in his neck and in the back of his head. He was the manager, but not even the damned dishwasher took his orders without an argument.

Rocks studied Louie with a cold, hard eye. "That ain't the best way to get results out of your employees."

"Fuck you, Daddy!"

"You can't take any kind of pressure at all, can you, son?" Rocks snorted. "I'd hate like hell to have had a fuckin' baby like you in the foxhole with me over in France during the war. You would have got everybody killed." Rocks went back out to the bar.

Louie picked up a glass and hurled it against the wall. It exploded into tiny pieces and left a wet mark on the sheetrock.

The dishwasher looked up at him with a combination of anger and fear. He slid off the dish chute, trying to seem casual, but he was edgy.

"Awright, awright, man. I'll mop the floor. Just chill out, will ya."

When Wayne tried to calm Louie down, it just made Louie angrier.

"Listen heah, White Boss, you—"

"Don't call me White Boss goddam it. Don't you have any fucking dignity?"

It was like that whenever Steve was in the place, which was often. Louie would withdraw to the kitchen and take out his frustration on the help. Steve never directly tried to order Louie around—if anything he ignored him—but there was something about Steve's presence that made Louie nauseous with anger.

Rocks, who knew nothing of Louie's history with Steve, couldn't understand Louie's attitude. "You're a fuckin' baby," was Rocks's only comment on Louie's behavior. "Any time you want out, I got your money for you."

But Louie had decided that he wasn't going to be pushed out of his own family's restaurant. Not to be replaced by the likes of Steve Wells. Nonetheless, Louie's interest in the cafe dwindled a little more each day, until he told himself he didn't care what Rocks did. Try to hang in long enough for the newspaper office to open, and when business took off as it should, his ten thousand would be worth thirty. In the meantime, he'd work at the cafe as if it were any other job, and he was just there to collect his paycheck.

THE CAFE took on three distinct personalities. During the lunch hour it was a sandwich takeout. In the evening it was a fried chicken and grilled T-bone place, with cornbread and overcooked vegetables. Late at night it was still a little Cajun, with red beans and rice, gumbo, jambalaya, and Louie's own Cajun lasagne, which he and Wayne and Alicia had concocted one night when business was slow and Wayne was too bored even to sleep.

Rocks now stayed from ten in the morning until ten at night, and Steve Wells hung around the bar all evening. The only time Louie felt any autonomy, any sense of a manager's control, was on the late night shift, after Rocks and Steve had left. During the remaining hours, the restaurant was someone else's, so Louie stayed away. He felt isolated not only from the restaurant but also from his family, since he now did his best to avoid them. When he did agree to come to Sunday dinner, the principal topic of conversation was everyone's disapproval of Alicia.

"You really sunk down low this time," said Gina, who looked as if she'd forgotten to brush her hair all week.

"I'm not sure about that," Louie said. "She's college-educated and pretty refined. I'd say she's got some class."

Gina's eyes squinted defensively. "Something tells me you want to add something more to that."

"Well, I guess I could," Louie said. "But I won't."

"Some nigger women ain't half bad to look at," said fat Rudy. "Better looking than some white women."

"You too?" Gina flared. "Why's everybody ganging up on *me*, for Chrissake? I ain't done nothing to nobody."

But it was Louie's mother, Bobbie, who was the most direct in attacking Louie. "You're disgracing all of us, you know."

"Ma, give it a rest."

"Don't you have any concern for the way we feel?"

"I love her, Ma. If you'd take a little time to get to know her, you might like her."

Bobbie shuddered. "I don't want to know her."

"Then forget it. It's my decision. Nobody else's."

In spite of his reflex defense of Alicia, Louie knew that their relationship was far from settled. He had come to realize that he was Alicia's pawn. She always expected more money than she had earned, and she constantly hinted that sooner or later Louie would have to confront her husband. If he really loved her, she said.

"Baby, you know I do. Don't you?"

"Sometimes I wonder."

"What makes you wonder?"

"When you get impatient with me."

"When is that?"

"Just a few minutes ago. You acted as if I didn't know the difference between a screwdriver and a tequila sunrise."

Louie tried to make a joke of it. "Hey, all I said was that a tequila sunrise wasn't—"

She cut him off. "I know what you said."

He watched her turn her back and carry a beer to a table. No nookie takes a toll, he nodded to himself. She seemed to live from one vaginal infection to the next, and Louie realized that they hadn't made love in over two weeks.

"We need to talk," she told him one night as they were closing.

"Sure. What's up?"

"I need an abortion."

"I thought you said you were on the pill?"

"Well, I guess they didn't work, did they."

That cost Louie three hundred and fifty dollars. He offered to bring her to the clinic, but she said she'd take care of it herself.

"But all those crazy protesters . . . you could get hurt."

Her smile was snide as she took the cash from him. "I guess I'll just have to take care of myself, won't I?"

Whenever he tried to see her during the day, she was busy. She said she had finally made the decision to go to medical school and was studying to take the Medical College Admission Test. She had a thick exam review book she brought to work with her and pretended to study in the kitchen every night, but she was really spending most of her time yakking with Wayne and Dwight, the dishwasher. Louie thought she acted more and more as if the world should worship her just because she was smart and capable. As if she were the first person in the history of the black race to be smart and capable. He noticed that she left the book at the cafe when she went home each morning.

She did pull him aside into the walk-in or the tiny bathroom in the kitchen to kiss him now and again, when he least expected it. And she left little love notes around. Sometimes she bought him something_an expensive pen, or a B.B. King CD. He couldn't call her neglectful; she had only made herself seem unreachable. And Louie needed a woman he could reach every day.

STEVE CAME IN very late one night with a dozen of his gambling buddies. Louie felt a black chill enter the place along with the November air. Several of them acted drunk, but Steve was the drunkest. He could barely stand up, and when he looked at Louie with his stupid grin, he seemed to have trouble focusing his eyes. He finally got himself perched on a bar stool.

"Don't I know you from someplace?" Steve asked.

"Yeah. I manage this place."

"No . . . I mean, somewhere else. A long time ago."

Louie tried to act as if Steve was not worth his time. He was taking glasses from a rubber rack and putting them on shelves behind the bar.

"I dunno, Steve. Maybe you do, and maybe you don't."

After a few moments, Steve stopped staring at Louie and laboriously swiveled around on his bar stool, nearly falling off as he did.

"I heard you was doing a big business at night. Shit, Bubba, this ain't half bad."

Louie didn't answer. The noise of the place spoke for itself. There were probably forty people there before Steve and his crowd came in. Louie noticed that the regulars were watching Steve's crowd.

Steve's voice rose when he spoke again. "Except for the fact that it's all fags. And niggers. And long-haired bums on drugs."

A silence descended over the place as the chatter turned to whispers. Louie picked up a rack of dirty glasses and escaped to the kitchen to plan how he should react. His palms were sweating and the back of his neck was tight and stiff. It was the moment he had dreaded; Rocks had finally sent Steve and a bunch of goons to start some trouble at the cafe and scare off Louie's late-night business. He was glad Alicia had taken the night off.

"You carry a gun?" he asked Wayne.

"No, White . . . Louie. Not unless I'm fixin' to walk into some trouble."

"And how do you know when you're seeing trouble?"

"I can usually tell by the look of things."

"Go out front and get me a Coke and tell me if you see anything like trouble." He thought he better get back on good terms with Wayne. "If you please, Darkie," he smiled.

Wayne smiled back. "Yahsuh, White Boss."

While Wayne was gone, Louie paced and sweated and tried to calm himself. At least he'd had a chance to think this time. If Alicia had been there, he would have had to act instantly, no matter how high the price.

Wayne was back in moments. "Looks cool to me. A little quiet, but cool."

Louie went to the kitchen door and looked through the window. Steve and his friends were gone, as were half the customers. Louie sighed deeply, but he sensed that trouble had only been postponed, not padlocked away.

"Start bringing your gun to work with you, okay?"

Wayne shook his head from side to side as he grimaced. "Look, Man, I don't get paid enough to be no gunfighter."

"I'm not talking about defending me," Louie said. "I'm talking about being ready in case you have to defend your own ass. I mean, the world is full of racists. You hear what I'm saying? Now start carrying your gun. Okay?"

LOUIE'S HUNCH was right. Steve started coming in three or four times a week late at night. He always had a few of his friends with him, and Louie watched with disgust as Steve bragged to them that he owned the place. Louie thought about how hard Rocks had worked all these years to open his own place. It was a crime to have brought in a bum like Steve to prop the place up when it didn't really need propping, at least not until Steve started to drive off the customers. And that was exactly what he was doing. After Steve's remark the week before—Louie realized now that Steve's drunkenness that night was an act—Louie's late night business was down by half.

One night Steve came into the kitchen, something he had never done before. Louie was reading the paper and ignored Steve.

"Hey. Mr. Bartender. We need some drinks out here."

Louie was tempted to tell him to get his own damned drinks, but he didn't want Steve to get into the habit of going behind the bar.

"I'll be right out."

Steve didn't leave. He stood in the doorway for several moments, then lumbered toward Louie and snatched the paper away from him. "I'm talking to you, boy," Steve said.

"Don't call me boy, Steve."

"Oh no? What are you gonna do about it . . . Boy?"

Louie had no control over the trembling that started inside him. He needed to be able to prepare his mind if he was going to fight Steve. He left the kitchen quickly and went out to the bar, certain that Steve wouldn't try to start anything out there.

"What can I get for you guys?" he asked the people at the bar. His trembling quieted some as he busied his hands making drinks, but his heartbeat quickened when Steve knocked over his bar stool trying to sit down.

"What do you think of my bartender here?" Steve said to his friends. "He's pretty good, isn't he?"

One of Steve's friends spoke up. "The best." The guy smirked. He had a narrow, ratlike face and a thin moustache that made him look distinctly seedier than the others. "The only thing wrong with this place is the niggers. Especially that nigger waitress."

A moment of damaging silence elapsed. Louie wasn't sure whether he should ignore these guys or argue with them until he noticed Alicia coming toward the bar with an order. He hoped that she had not heard the remark.

"Two mai tais and a Bud," Alicia said.

"You know, Harry, I have to agree," said Steve, his eyes holding on Louie. "There ain't no reason in the world why we need a nigger waitress in a place that could be all-white."

Alicia's eyes opened wide and fastened themselves on Louie. Louie tried to sound calm, but when he opened his mouth, his voice cracked like a pretzel. "If you don't like the help, Steve, you can go somewhere else."

All of them smiled a moment at each other before they hollered with laughter. Then they watched Alicia. Alicia glared back at them as Louie made the mai-tais and popped open a Bud longneck for her. She took the drinks without looking at him and started toward her tables.

"Uppity," ratface Harry said.

"She happens to be well educated and very intelligent," Louie said, hoping it was loud enough for Alicia to hear.

"Worst kind," said Steve. "Louie, old boy, looks to me like it's time to get rid of her."

Louie opened his mouth to speak but closed it quickly, realizing that he might only stammer. He forced himself to speak anyway. "I'm in charge of the hiring here," Louie said, surprised at the sudden steadiness in his voice and in his mind.

"I know," said Steve. "That's why I'm ordering *you* to fire her instead of ordering your daddy to do it."

"I'm not firing her," Louie said. His voice was almost calm. "And I won't have you ordering my daddy to do a damned thing." He placed his hands on the bar and leaned a few inches toward Steve. "In fact, I was thinking of putting Miss Alicia on days as *head* waitress."

"Ooooh, I don't think so, Bubba."

Louie smiled. "You don't own this place, and you don't run it. Daddy and me still own more of this place than you."

Steve sat back slightly, his eyes and mouth in a hard grin. "We'll see about that tomorrow."

Louie nodded. "Okay, Steve. I'll be waiting to hear." He was sure Rocks would not consider selling more of the place to Steve. It was bad enough to have the guy holding forty percent. Nor could Louie imagine Steve putting up more money just to prove a point.

Louie went into the kitchen and took refuge in the walk-in. He was panting, pumped up, proud of himself for facing Steve down. But Alicia came in moments later, her face furrowed with anger.

"You expect me to work under these conditions?" she shrieked.

"Hey, he told me to fire you and I told him to fuck off. Didn't you hear me?"

Alicia handed him her order pad and stormed out, slamming the two-way kitchen door against the wall. It stuck open. Louie watched her continue through the dining room to the outside door and disappear.

He started out of the kitchen but did not try to catch up with her. From his seat at the bar, Steve looked from Louie to the retreating form of Alicia and back to Louie.

"God damn, Boy. That didn't take no time at all once you put your mind to it. Ain't that right?"

Steve's friends laughed.

Louie turned all the lights on bright. "Party's over. I'm closing for the night." He went around to the tables and started to collect dirty dishes but then decided to leave them for Rocks.

As the last of the customers filed out, Steve and his friends finished their drinks and headed toward the door.

"You're the boss, Hoss," Steve said, still smirking. "If you say it's quitting time, then quitting time it is."

Louie said nothing, but when he went back into the kitchen, he punched his fist through the sheetrock wall.

IV

After Alicia had stayed gone for a week, Steve and his buddies stopped coming in at night. Louie moped around the place in a trance, too sapped even to feel angry. The late-night business had dwindled to less than a hundred dollars a night, so Louie started closing at two instead of staying open until six in the morning.

He had a history, he reminded himself, of falling in love with women whose personalities and lives were too complicated. The maddening part was that things were always so good at first. The older he got, the better each venture began, and the worse it ended. Alicia hurt the worst yet.

The next time Louie did see Steve was when Steve called a staff meeting. The three of them sat at a corner table. Steve drank a bourbon, Rocks drank a tonic water with lemon, and Louie, his head swimming with the irony of having a total amateur like Steve Wells calling the shots, drank water. Louie noticed that his father was quiet, looking out the window rather than at Steve.

"We're changing everything," Steve announced. "I figure if we change up the format a little, we can get a whole different crowd in here. Make it kind of a sports grill."

"A sports grill?" Louie shook his head. "So a bunch of rednecks can piss and moan about the Auburn-Alabama game?"

"Beats the hell out of the crowd coming in here now."

Louie laughed. "Thanks to you, Steve, there isn't any crowd that comes in here now."

"We'll change the dinner menu, too, and go straight Eye-talian. All you can eat spaghetti and meatballs on Monday nights to go along with the football game."

Again Louie shook his head. "Another spaghetti joint? Birmingham really needs one more shitty Italian restaurant."

"That's what my friends want," Steve said, opening his folded hands a moment then reclosing them, faking patience.

"I think he's right," Rocks said. "Your mother makes the best lasagne in Alabama, and your grandmother—"

Louie stood up. "Do whatever you want. I really don't care any-more."

A few minutes later, Rocks came into the kitchen, where Louie was helping Wayne peel potatoes.

"Son, I wish—"

"Daddy, how much of this place does Steve own now?"

Rocks looked surprised. "What the hell are you talking about? He owns forty percent. That's what I sold him. Half my share."

Louie closed his eyes. "Sickening."

"I wish to hell you'd try to get along with him. Even an idiot can have a good idea once in awhile. This Italian thing might fly."

Louie took consolation from hearing Rocks call Steve an idiot. It was a start. Maybe they could hold on long enough for the newspaper office to get built, then buy Steve out. Steve would want ten times what he put in, and he wouldn't have lifted a finger doing any work. But getting him out was worth just about any price, Louie told himself.

Louie could tell that Rocks had something else on his mind. "Yeah?"

"I heard that waitress friend of yours quit again."

Louie mashed his tongue against the roof of his mouth and said nothing. At least Rocks had not called her a nigger. Not with Wayne standing right there.

"I wish she'd quit before I let Steve in on this place," Rocks went on. "I only got him involved so's I could come up with the money to buy *you* out. Since you seemed to be saying it was her over me."

"Well, she's gone now, Daddy. Are you satisfied?"

Rocks waited a moment before he said anything. "I just wish it'd been you that ran her off instead of Steve. Now he thinks he's calling all the shots."

"Well? Isn't he?"

Rocks looked at Louie with a face that wavered between hard and soft. "I guess he is, if you're gonna toss in the towel without even giving him a fight."

WHEN ALICIA called a little while later, Louie was glad he was the one who answered the phone.

"I have to move out," she said. "Right away. Can you put me up somewhere?"

He wasn't sure how he felt to hear from her, but he tried to sound happy. "Sure. Hey, that's great. You're finally doing it."

"He'll come looking for me. And he probably won't be alone."

Louie thought about Rocks's gun, hidden under the bar. The idea of shooting Reginald gave Louie an adrenaline rush like he'd never known. It was time to prove that he really did have whatever he felt he lacked when a guy like Steve Wells threw his books into a shit-filled commode.

"I don't care if he brings the National Guard in here after us. I won't let him get near you," he asserted.

He felt her eyes over the phone and pictured them as they grew large with tears. "Sometimes I think you really do love me, Louie."

The sadness of love ballooned in his heart. He'd always been a romantic, and he'd always assumed he was fated to die in a love-related scenario much like the one that seemed to be writing itself now. Either love this woman right, he told himself, or be honest enough to tell her you just don't have the guts.

"Can you meet me in fifteen minutes at Five Points?" he asked her.

"That's where I am right now. At Rube Burrow's."

Rocks and Steve still sat at the corner table, planning the new menu. Louie found the pistol on the shelf behind the bar, still hidden under the stack of counter towels. He checked to make sure it was loaded and that he knew how to work the safety, then he stuffed the pistol inside his shirt and headed for the door.

"I'm taking the night off, Daddy. I'd say it's Steve's turn to put in a night's work."

"I can't do it," he heard Steve say to Rocks. "I already got plans." Louie smiled to himself. That was one way to keep the bastard out of the cafe; make him think if he showed up he'd have to work. When Louie got to Rube Burrow's, he found Alicia sitting at the bar talking to two guys. They were buying her drinks. She held one in her hand—it looked like a mai tai, their private drink. A second drink sat on the bar near her elbow.

Louie's heart began to rap hard inside his throat. "Louie! You're here. This is Daryl and this is—what's your name again?"

"LeShon."

Louie was relieved that neither of them was Reginald. Daryl was white, burly, black-bearded, with a clean-shaven skull. He wore a gold hoop in his left ear lobe. LeShon was black and stood with his hands jammed into the pockets of his baggy pants. He wore sunglasses and a beret. "Have a drink," Alicia said, laughing. "Daryl's buying."

"No thanks. I thought maybe you were ready to go. I need to get back to work if you aren't." The joviality drained from her face. She said nothing, but her eyes told him that pushy was not what she was looking for in a man just then.

"These are classmates of mine," she said. "A year from now, we may all be in medical school together."

"Congratulations," Louie said, trying to stand against the bar in a way that hid the bulge in his shirt. Alicia drained the first glass and started on the second. She winked at Louie.

"Since you're in such a rush."

Daryl and LeShon had not taken their eyes off Louie since he'd walked into the place, and Louie suspected that they had noticed his bulging shirt. He felt like a total amateur. He watched Alicia drain her second drink.

Louie set a ten-dollar bill on the counter and nodded to the two men as he and Alicia walked away, arm-in-arm. Very cool, Louie decided. When they got in the car and hugged, her hand brushed across his shirt-front. She unbuttoned the shirt and laughed when she saw the gun.

"You know how to shoot that thing?" she asked.

"I heard it comes naturally."

She laughed again. It was a drunken laugh that made him sad, but he laughed with her anyway. They went to the Hyatt downtown, the hotel where they first made love. She insisted that they shower together, something they had never done. Watching her undress, Louie was aware that she had brought only her purse, which made him think this was hardly a case of moving out. Unless she had already stored all her clothes elsewhere. Or perhaps she had felt compelled to get away quickly with only the clothes on her back. The water spilled over Alicia's beautiful, bony face and shoulders, and he reached to catch her as she began to fall.

She laughed maniacally. "Isn't this fun?"

"How much have you had to drink?"

"Don't be a downer, Louie. My Dearest."

"Look, I want you back in the restaurant."

"Never. Not after what happened last time."

"It doesn't do any good to fight Steve over something like that. And he's not the important one anyway, it's my daddy. You know that. It's not insults we should be letting ourselves get worked up about. We're bigger than insults, aren't we?" Louie's breath came faster as he felt a surge of conviction and wisdom. "We gotta show them that we're at peace with the world, not at war. We've got to show them we're above the shit they want to drag us down to wallow in with them."

"I don't want to think about it."

"I know. But I want you with me. All the time. If Reginald is going to come after you, you're going to have to stay with me while I'm working. And if I'm working, you can go through the motions of working, too."

"I've got the M-CAT coming up. I was hoping you'd just kind of take care of me while I study, baby." Louie decided to be honest with her and tell her everything that was going through his mind.

"Daddy's ready to buy out my share of the cafe. He's got the cash from Steve to do it, and I'm ready to get out. If I bring you back there to work, baby, it won't take an hour before those two are in the kitchen asking me how much. And would that be cash, check, or money order?"

"Shit."

"Bring your books and study at the restaurant. That'll really piss them off." Louie laughed. When he looked at her again, her eyes were open. The water streamed over her like a jungle waterfall.

"You said Alicia isn't your only name. Why do you have other names?"

She laughed again, her eyes wide and wild. "Because I'm an *actress*, baby. I never know from one day to the next who I want to be."

"I think they have a name for that in medicine. What is it, crazy? Something like that?"

She sobered. "No, it's for things like bill collectors. If somebody calls my house looking for Lula, or Mimi, or May or Barbara, I know exactly which bill collector it is."

"Or ex-boyfriend?"

She smiled again. "Or current boyfriend."

"Don't joke about that."

"I'm sorry. Let's kiss and make up." She tilted her head back into the water and drank him in as they kissed. She was the most beautiful woman he'd ever seen, he told himself, and he was ready to die for her if he had to.

NEXT MORNING, Louie left while Alicia was still asleep and drove to his parents' house to gather enough clothes and toothpaste and shaving cream to last him a few days.

"What are you doing?" Rocks had snuck up behind him.

"Taking a break."

"Where are you going? Who's going to work tonight?"

"I am."

"Where were you last night? No, don't tell me. Let me guess. Shacked up with a nigger witch?"

Louie's anger simmered but he promised himself to remain calm. "Daddy, I happen to be in love with that woman. If you can't use a better word than nigger, please don't even mention her."

Rocks shook his head. "I thought she was goddam gone."

"Well, she's back. And I'm glad. In fact, we're going to live together as soon as I can find us a place. And I'm planning to give her back her job. If she'll take it."

Rocks looked alarmed. "No! Absolutely not!"

"It's not your call, Daddy."

"Why do you work so hard to disgrace your—?"

Louie slammed the bedroom door on him before Rocks could finish his sentence. He drove back to the hotel, stopping first to pick up some McDonald's breakfast. He undressed in the room before he woke her up, and they ate in the nude. They spoke little but smiled every time they looked at each other. Louie realized once again how little it took in this life to make him happy.

They spent the day apartment-hunting but found nothing. Landlords looked at them with a variety of hatreds and said that the apartments advertised in the paper that morning were already rented. They inquired about twenty apartments and were actually shown a few, but none of the places they could have taken that same day were ones they wanted to live in. Louie stopped to get takeout Mexican and drove Alicia back to the hotel.

"Louie, why do you love me?"

"Christ, let's talk about something answerable, okay?"

"Is it because you think I'm smart? And ambitious?"

"I like that in you. I'll admit it."

"If I become a doctor, we'll be able to live pretty well, don't you think?"

"I guess so. I hadn't thought about it much. Isn't this the best tamale you ever had?"

"Louie, what if I told you I really am ambitious. And smart. But all that was on hold right now? And that I had all this other stuff I have to straighten out right now before I can really get down to business? Would you still love me?"

"Only if you came back to work tonight."

"I'm serious, Louie."

"Help me for the next few nights, and then we'll have enough money to take care of both of us for awhile."

Her smile was slower than usual, but when it began to bloom, it glowed. "White Boy," she said. "There's almost something different about you today."

When they went into work that night, Louie's entire family—brothers, sister, grandparents, aunts, and uncles he saw only on Christmas Eve when they all got together to eat Italian sausage—were waiting to talk to him. In their faces Louie saw everything from amusement to alarm. Alicia looked at no one and went straight to the kitchen.

Bobbie's eyes were puffed and red. She couldn't summon a voice to speak without starting to cry. And Rocks, who was operating from the other end of the spectrum of persuasive technique, ordered Louie straight out to fire Alicia and to stop seeing her. Somehow Rocks had found out that she was married. The consensus was that Alicia, in spite of her so-called education—or, more likely, because of it—was hideously immoral. And that she wasn't educated at all, no matter what she claimed. She was just putting on airs. It had nothing to do with race, they all claimed. It was values and morals. Black people thought differently from the rest of us, Rocks's father insisted. Alicia had obviously been a bad influence on Louie, trying to turn him colored. It would only get worse. As Grandpa droned on, Louie went behind the bar and replaced the gun where he had found it. He told himself it was a good idea to have a gun, and that he should buy himself one at the earliest opportunity.

Louie found the scene comical at first. It was a simple matter of his being a little more enlightened than the rest of his family. There were good and bad people in every crowd, he tried to explain. But as his opinions met with worried shakes of heads, Louie realized that the situation was more complex than he wanted to admit, and that it would take years, if not centuries, to undo all their irrational conditioning.

"I'll think about it," he promised them.

Now Bobbie's mother and father each took one of Louie's hands. "Don't just think about it," they pleaded. "Promise me right now that you'll tell her no," said Grandpa Adriano.

"Luigi, Luigi, Luigi. She just cause you the big trouble," Grandma Sophia went on. "She break-a you heart."

Based on what had already transpired between him and Alicia, Louie knew that was a distinct possibility.

"Thank you, Nonna. I appreciate your advice."

They left, Rocks and Bobbie with them, but no one seemed satisfied. Louie found Alicia in the kitchen, sitting quietly with Wayne. She seemed more lost and lonely than Louie had ever seen her, as if she could sense not only the pressure Louie was dealing with but also his potential for caving in. It was a potential he had not considered while he argued with his family, only when he saw Alicia face-to-face.

Louie was surprised when Rocks came back alone a half hour later. "Son, there's one more thing . . ."

"It's finished, Daddy. No more discussion."

"Son, there's something you gotta know, wheter you want to or not. That gal ain't no college student. They never heard of her at Auburn or Alabama. Not at UAB, Samford, Birmingham-Southern, Miles, Jeff State. None of them. She's a fuckin' liar, son. I just wanted you to know that." Rocks stared at his son a moment, turned, and left.

Back in the kitchen with Alicia, Louie's heart gnawed at him as if he had a rat inside.

"By the way," she said. "I heard what your father said. He's right. I didn't go to UAB or Samford or Jeff State or Birmingham-Southern. I went to Montevallo. On scholarship. I guess he didn't bother to check there."

Louie smiled at her and tried to feel good about things. But he just couldn't quite manage it. He almost asked her what her college name was.

ABOUT NINE that night, Steve and a dozen of his friends came in. Steve set a carton on the bar and began showing his friends, not Louie, the new menu. Louie felt a belt tighten around his neck. He tried to appear calm but he ached as if someone had punched him.

Steve and his pals seemed uninterested in Louie, except to order drinks. No one tried to engage his eyes, no one smirked when he served them. They were the only customers, so Louie went back to the kitchen. Wayne was napping, and Alicia was actually studying. Louie bent to kiss the back of her neck.

When he went back out front, he saw only Steve and two of his friends at the bar. Louie looked around and found Harry in the back room shooting pool with another of Steve's buddies, a big guy with long, unkempt hair.

"This is a private pool table," Louie said quickly.

Harry smiled. "This is a private game."

Louie felt his trembles coming on, but he held firm. "I guess you don't understand. You see, I own that pool table, not the restaurant."

Harry and Louie locked eyes for a moment, then Harry and his friend stood their cue sticks against the wall. Harry spread the plastic cover back over the table.

"Happy?"

Louie felt bolder. "No. But a little less pissed-off."

Harry laughed and nodded toward the mattress against the wall.

"That the workbench you and the Mau-mau use? Silk sheets? Must be good."

Then Steve was in the doorway right beyond Louie. "God damn it, Harry. Will you leave this guy alone?"

Harry and the longhair laughed as they went back toward the bar. Louie waited for Steve to leave, but he didn't. He looked very serious as he studied Louie.

"Can I have a word with you? Man to man, sort of?"

Louie didn't know what to make of Steve's seemingly conciliatory demeanor, and he almost laughed. But he could not resist the urge to find out what was going on.

"Sure. What's on your mind?"

"It's about your dad. He's one of my dearest friends, I guess you probably know by now."

"No, I didn't know."

"Well, he is. I think the world of Rocks. Me and a whole bunch of other folks, too. When he first come to me about buying into this restaurant, I wasn't interested. But now that I got a little taste of it, I believe this is just what I been looking for. And I ain't got nobody but Rocks to thank, you hear what I'm saying?" Steve paused, studying Louie.

"Sure."

"I just wanted to see if they ain't some way I can help you two work out some of your differences. I hate to see a boy and his daddy have a falling out like you two."

Again, Louie had to fight off the urge to laugh. "I'm not sure I know what you're getting at, Steve."

"Oh, that business with that black waitress. I know she's a good looking young lady and probably a lot of fun for you and all. But your daddy's from the old school, you know, and he don't understand what's going on between the two of you. I sure wish you could find a way to let her go her way and you go yours and take a big load off your daddy's mind." Steve paused and creased his face even more earnestly. "It ain't like you couldn't find yourself a nice white girl."

Louie sighed. "Steve, I appreciate your concern, but I think I can handle my own love life."

Steve waited a minute, then broke a small grin. "Well, how about this? How about if I gave you six thousand dollars for your share of this place, and that way you and your mistress, or whatever you call her, can go do your thing somewheres else so your daddy don't have to know about it?"

"How about twenty thousand? I might consider that."

Steve's smile grew. "Bubba, it ain't like your share's worth that much."

"Twenty's my price. And I'd rather sell my share to my father, not to you."

"Your daddy ain't got the money to give you shit, Bubba. I'm trying to tell you this is the only deal in town." He nodded, his smile never flagging. "Well, it ain't the only deal. I'm sure you could probably come up with a whole lot worser one. If you put your mind to it."

Louie started for the door. "Thanks, but I only have one price in mind. It'll go up before it goes down."

Louie went into the men's room to take a leak and think about the laugh he'd held in during Steve's speech.

V

The Cafe was serene in the way that a restaurant void of customers seems at peace with itself. Louie felt assured in his sense of confidence. It wasn't just a surge but a solid sense of himself after he'd stood up to Harry about his pool table and Steve about his price. And now that he had had a few minutes to think about it, he was glad his price was not forthcoming. He'd put too much into this place, he and Rocks both, to turn it over to an outsider. What if Steve had agreed to the twenty thousand, Louie thought now. Thank Christ he didn't; that would have meant turning majority ownership of his father's place over to Steve. Louie had planned to sell his share to Rocks, not Steve.

In the kitchen, both Wayne and Alicia dozed, Wayne leaning against the wall in his chair, Alicia with her head on her folded arms on the serving board of the steam table. It was a funny business, Louie thought as he watched them. Busy and prosperous one week or month, dead the next. He wanted to touch Alicia's back and kiss her hair, but he let her sleep instead.

The phone startled them all awake. Louie went out front to answer it. The men at the bar watched him instead of the TV.

"Alice there?"

Louie had to turn down the music to hear. "Who?"

"Alice. She there?"

"You mean Alicia?"

"Yeah."

Louie hurt as he opened the kitchen door and motioned to her. She hesitated, knit her brow to ask who. Louie shrugged. When she took the phone, she waved Louie away and spoke in whispers. Steve and his friends alternately watched her and Louie. Louie pretended to watch the TV. She hung up and sauntered back to the kitchen. Louie waited a minute before he went back after her. Wayne was asleep again.

"What's up?"

She shook her head. "He's coming to pick me up."

"Who?"

"Reginald."

"I won't let him."

"Louie, you have no idea—"

"I won't let him. I told you I'd take care of you, and that's what I'm going to do."

"Louie, you don't understand. It's more complicated than I can—"

"Do you love him?"

She looked away, drumming her fingers on the sideboard where her hand rested. She no longer wore bracelets and rings the way she used to, he noticed.

"Do you or not? If you don't, I'll figure out a way to get rid of him."

"Yes and no," she said.

Louie felt the deep stab all over, mostly in his mind. His body and mind cried, but he managed to keep his hot eyes dry. "What about me?"

"That's the problem," she said. "I love you, too."

It wasn't the answer Louie wanted to hear, but he decided it was good enough. He went into the pool room to use the phone. He called the Southside precinct and asked to talk to his Uncle Willy, who was a night desk sergeant. He didn't particularly like Willy, but he felt he had no choice.

"Hey, how ya doing? Great, great. Daddy's doing fine. Keeps saying we need to get you in here for supper some night. Yeah, I saw you down here one time, but that was six months ago. You ain't been back since. Yeah, come back anytime. And bring Aunt Millie. I'll get the cook to make something good for you. Look, could you have one of your guys keep an eye on the place? I think I'm fixing to have a rough crowd in here tonight. I mean, just have him park across the street and keep an eye on things. Thanks, Willy. Yeah, we'll all come over some time soon. Tell Aunt Millie I said hi. Okay. Thanks."

A few minutes later, Louie noticed a cruiser parked across the street. He made himself a drink, just to keep his confidence at the right level and to calm the shakes, which had already started in his heart and were trying to start in his hands.

Back in the kitchen, Alicia talked with Wayne about somebody they both knew. She did not seem upset. Her M-CAT review book lay open on the counter.

"I need a drink," she said. She got up and went out to the bar.

"Did you bring your gun?" Louie asked Wayne.

"No." He looked pained by the question.

"Did you know that Alicia's married?"

"Well . . . yeah."

"You know her husband?"

"I know who he is. I don't really know him."

"Is he bad?"

"I dunno. I ain't never heard he was."

"Big?"

"Not really."

"Think I could take him?"

Wayne smiled. "I dunno, White Boss. I never seen you fight. I dunno how bad *you* be."

Alicia came back with her drink. Louie went out front to watch the street. Steve sat at the bar with Harry studying a racing form, and the three other friends sat at a booth.

"You let the help drink while they're on the clock?" Steve asked.

Louie was wired, combative. "She's a little nervous. Studying for her exam to get into medical school. I told her she could have a drink if she wanted one."

Steve and Harry laughed. "That's right. I forgot they got nigger doctors now, don't they?" Harry said.

Louie said nothing.

"You could grow bananas in Alaska before I'd let a nigger doctor cut on me," Steve said.

"If I talked about them the way you do," said Louie, "I wouldn't want a black coming at me with a scalpel, either."

Steve stared at Louie a moment, then glanced around the restaurant. "Business looks a little slack. I told you a long time ago that having a nigger waitress was bad for business. But you keep bringing her back."

"Business is slack because you ran my customers off."

Steve's smile was suddenly twice as wide as his face. "I don't see it that way, Bubba" said Steve. "I believe me and you has got a different philosophy of how to run a decent restaurant."

"That's for damned sure." Louie made the mistake of glancing out the window to make sure the police car was still there.

Steve glanced outside, too, then turned back to Louie with a smile. "I believe that's Tommy Moseley out there. I bet he's taking a break."

Louie wondered where Steve had stowed the friendliness he'd shown earlier when they talked in the pool room.

Steve turned toward one of his friends. "Go out there and tell Tommy to come in here and have a drink with us. Or a cup of coffee or something." Steve took out a money clip and peeled off a fifty dollar bill. "Or go have himself a little supper. He don't need to be sitting over there when they's all kinds of criminals running around loose tonight."

Louie's throat tightened as he watched Steve's friend cross the street, speak to the cop, hand him the money. The cop pulled away, and Steve's friend came back inside.

"Yeah, cops got it good, don't they?" Steve said.

ALICIA PACED in the kitchen. Louie watched her a moment as she sipped her drink.

"Where's Wayne?"

"Bathroom, I guess."

"Are you really going to go with Reginald?"

"Yes. I have to. And you don't need someone like me in your life, Louie. Believe me."

"But I can help you through med—"

She looked at him, crying, and picked up her M-CAT book. "This?" She tossed the book into the trash can by the steam table. "That's not for real. That was just so you'd put up with me."

But Louie didn't care anymore; he told himself he wanted her no matter what she was not. He went to her to take her into his arms. She cried against his shoulder.

"I'm so fucked up, Louie. I'm hopeless. You don't need me fucking you up, too. I've already caused you more trouble than I ever meant to."

Steve poked his head through the kitchen door and smiled. "Y'all got some company out here."

Louie and Alicia looked at each other, then Louie looked back at Steve, who remained at the door. Alicia pulled away and tossed back the last of her drink. Louie could see by the way she looked at the empty glass that she really wanted another.

"They're waiting," Steve said.

Louie's insides rocked him like the sea. His vision blurred with hatred as he watched Steve's smile grow.

"I heard you, Steve."

"Don't say I didn't offer to help you out," Steve said. "You coulda been out of here with cash in hand an hour ago." Steve opened the door wide and held it.

Alicia squeezed Louie's arm and headed out of the kitchen. Louie saw four black men standing beside the bar. He hesitated a moment, then ran after her. "Wait."

One of the blacks stepped in his way and stopped Louie with a shove that almost knocked him down. Alicia did not see it; she led the way as they all filed out the door. As soon as they were gone, Steve and his friends broke into an immense laughter.

Despite his resolve not to, Louie started to tremble, more violently than in his worst nightmares. Steve put a hand on Louie's shoulder, and when Louie knocked it off, he also knocked a rack of glasses off the end of the bar and onto the floor. The crashing glass flew everywhere. Louie bent to pick up some of the broken glass, thinking he could use a large shard to defend himself if Steve touched him again.

"Don't you touch that glass," Steve roared. "That's what that nigger out in the kitchen is here for! In fact, I'll go get him right now."

Louie made a move after Steve, but Harry stuck out his leg and tripped Louie up. Louie sprawled on the floor for a moment, near the broken glass. He sprang to his feet and lunged into Harry with his head, knocking Harry off his stool and sending him sliding across the hardwood floor. Harry was back on his feet in a single motion and now came toward Louie with a knife. Steve and two others grabbed Louie, pinning his arms. Harry grabbed the hair on the top of Louie's head and yanked it back, exposing the entire length of Louie's neck. He held the blade sideways against it.

"You just don't know how to act around white people anymore, do you?" Harry said in a spray of spit.

Louie, to his amazement, was no longer trembling. He watched Harry's hard, smiling eyes, and felt the stiffness of metal against his skin.

"Go ahead and cut me, motherfucker," Louie said. "I don't much give a shit at this point."

In a few moments, Harry put his knife back in his pocket. Steve released Louie's arms.

Louie went back behind the bar to find Rocks's gun. He wouldn't shoot anyone; he'd only order Steve and his gang out of the bar.

But the gun was gone. Steve, laughing again, took the pistol out of his pocket and tossed it to Louie.

"It ain't got no bullets. I didn't want you to hurt no one. Such as yourself."

They left. Louie watched them until they had gotten in Steve's car and driven around the corner.

Wayne came out of the kitchen with a broom and dustpan. He looked terrified. "Are you okay, Louie?"

"No."

"Am I fired?"

Louie's rage leapt out of him. Where the hell were Wayne and his gun when Harry was about to slice Louie's throat? "Of course you're fired! What the fuck you think?"

Wayne looked at Louie with a ripple of disgust mixed with perfect understanding. He let the broom and dustpan he carried drop to the floor. "Whatever you say." Wayne sauntered toward the door. He still walked like a fat man, Louie thought, even though he'd lost at least twenty pounds since he came to work at Cafe Roma.

LOUIE DROVE until daybreak, down I-65 to Montgomery, where he turned around and headed back to Birmingham, bypassing the city and continuing north toward Huntsville. He stopped outside Cullman for gas. His self-hatred had never been heavier on his heart nor more acid in his gut. Once he had gassed up, he felt no inclination to drive further. He took a room in a motel beside the expressway where a yard full of tractor trailer trucks, many of their engines running, lowed like a corral full of cattle. As he lay in bed, the growl of the diesel engines comforted him. He dozed off, imagining himself as a trucker out on the open road, one who never had to come home if he didn't want to. He was neither awake nor asleep, only drifting, but what he felt seemed almost like peace. He slept all day, awakened only once by the maid who wanted to clean up the room. By the time he awoke, it was nearly nightfall. He lay in bed, feeling the weight of dread once again settle over him. What was done was done, he tried to tell himself. There was no correcting past failures. The best he could hope for was to avoid future ones.

He checked out of the motel and headed for Birmingham. He couldn't possibly continue working at the cafe, so he decided to visit some of his restaurant friends around town and find himself a job.

He got the news at the first place where he stopped. He was talking with Donnie Phillips, the manager at Michael's.

"Sorry about your place."

Louie was embarrassed. So, the scene the night before was already the subject of restaurant gossip around town. He played dumb. "What do you mean?"

"The fire and all. I heard nobody got hurt."

Now Louie's heart began to beat so hard it seemed it might bolt from his chest. "What are you talking about?"

"You don't know? Christ, your placed burned down last night." Donnie lowered his voice. "They say a bunch of blacks did it. Somebody saw three or four black guys around there just before the fire started."

Louie immediately drove toward the cafe, which was just a few blocks east. Sure enough, the place was a charred, gutted shell of brick. The smell of smoke lingered like bad breath, and Louie found himself trembling for real as he tried to picture the beautiful oak bar, his pool table, his expensive stereo. The whole goddam thing in ashes, and no insurance.

Wayne? he wondered. Dwight? Alicia or her husband, Louie wondered. Thirty years old and now all you own is a fifteen-year-old car. And you goddam near owned a slit throat.

Louie drove to the police station to find out what had happened. When he told them who he was, a sergeant came out from his office. He was a big guy who looked almost like Steve.

"We been looking for you. What happened last night?"

"I honestly couldn't tell you."

"We talked to Rocks and he don't know nothing either. He thinks some blacks might have done it, though."

"It doesn't surprise me that he'd think that."

Louie told them what little he knew. The motel part of his story was easy to confirm—the desk clerk and the maid at the motel in Cullman verified his story when the police called. But the cops still wanted to know where Louie was between closing time and dawn, when he checked into the motel. Louie had no answer. The cops wanted to know where Alicia, Wayne, and Dwight lived. Louie told them he didn't know—that their addresses and telephone numbers were on a pad of paper in the cafe. He assumed the pad had been burned along with everything else.

"Now you and this Alicia Hargrove had a thing going, is that correct?" the sergeant asked.

Louie didn't like the tone of the questioning. "Am I a suspect or something?" he asked.

"We ain't sure yet it's arson. Yet. At this point it just looks like somebody left the stove on. But it coulda been intentional." The sergeant paced behind the chair where Louie sat. "Now tell us about this Alicia Hargrove. Your dad said you two had a thing going?"

"Yeah..."

"Are you hiding her somewhere?"

Louie had never before been questioned by the police. He felt the sweat on his temples and knew he must have looked guilty of something. "Look," he said. "I wouldn't burn my own family's place down. We didn't have any insurance."

The two detectives questioning him looked at each other.

"That ain't quite true, kid," one of them said. "The place had insurance."

Louie shook his head. "No. I tried to get my father to buy insurance, and he claimed there was never enough money."

One of the detectives flipped through his notebook. When he came to the page he was looking for, he passed the notebook to the sergeant.

"A hundred and fifty thousand dollars worth," the sergeant said. "That's just the fire insurance."

Louie was confused; why wouldn't Rocks have told him there was insurance?

"It's in the name of Steve Wells. He's your old man's partner, right?"

It all came clear to Louie. "Yeah. He's Dad's partner all right."

LOUIE LEFT THE police station angrier than he'd ever been in his life. He wondered if Steve had included Rocks on the policy, or if the insurance was in his name alone. And who, exactly, had Steve hired to torch the place?

Or had Wayne just walked out the door and forgotten he'd left a burner on? If that was the case, the fire was Louie's own damned fault for not closing the place down properly when he took off.

At home, Louie found Rocks a defeated man, sunk deep into the couch that the bank now owned, in the den Rocks had built himself but that the bank now also owned. Louie had never seen him so quiet or so calm. They sat in silence for what seemed to Louie like an hour. They would have to move out of their home, he assumed, and Rocks, who should have been rich and retired by now, would be back tending bar in some hole so that they could rent a dumpy apartment.

"I told you that gal was trouble," Rocks said, nearly in a whisper.

Louie bowed his head and said nothing.

Rocks started to get up, but the effort made him settle back into the cushions. "Son, son, son. Look what you made me do."

"What do you mean, *I* made you do? What did you do?"

Rocks said nothing. He didn't have to; Louie understood everything just by the look in his father's eyes, and the cold sweat of total loss crawled over him.

"How can you say I made you do it, Daddy? That's the craziest thing I've ever heard."

"You wouldn't listen. You're too pig-headed to listen."

Pig-headed, Louie thought. He wanted to laugh. What a tag for Rocks to pin on anybody.

"So you decapitate someone to cure their headache? Is that what you're saying?"

"Don't piss me off, Son. You already caused enough damage. I hope to hell you learned a lesson."

STEVE, TO LOUIE'S utter amazement, did share the insurance money, even though it was Steve who had initiated the policy and made all the payments. The bank took most of the money right off the top, which left Rocks and Bobbie with the original sixty thousand. And they didn't lose their house. Neither Rocks nor Steve offered Louie his ten thousand.

Louie wanted to leave, go to Florida, start his life over, but he didn't have the money to move across town, let alone to another state. And by the time he was working again and had put aside a few thousand dollars, his life seemed almost normal. He told himself he had to stay around to help support his parents. Rocks had taken another job as a bartender, but he couldn't put in the hours he used to.

Life was pretty strained at the Romano home for several months, but eventually everything settled down and the family stopped treating Louie like a disease. And when Rocks got a chance to buy another place, this time in one of the malls south of town, Louie, against his better judgment, went in with him.

Rocks picked out the name. "What do you say we call the place On the Rocks?" he asked Louie.

"Whatever you say, Daddy."

It was the old movie: Rocks tended bar, Louie was general manager, Bobbie was bookkeeper, and various family members mismanaged various functions of the restaurant until Louie fired them and Rocks rehired them. And when Wayne showed up one afternoon looking for a job as a cook, Louie found it impossible to turn him away.

Business was not bad at the mall.

Desserts

Epilogue

Dear Theodora,

Here are two more clips from our esteemed local newspaper. I'm just about convinced that it's the same guy writing both columns. With the restaurants around here, maybe you have to be essentially schizophrenic to write reviews.

Here's my latest evidence. Tell Michael I said hello and that he's the only man I know who could begin to deserve the likes of you. Elroy says hi, as do Hamlet, the Great Dane, and Omar, the Persian Cat.

Boomers
640 Oxbow Road
879-0001

This is one of our city's only see-and-be-seen places, and I see half the town's up-and-comers here every afternoon at the impeccably appointed bar, with Dino at the helm. The man can, as I've mentioned more than once in this space, make a martini. The streetside plays its dramas just outside the wide windows, and inside, the studs jocky for position while the princesses suggest their receptiveness with tossed heads and shimmering shoulders. I can't say that the aura of this bar is not wanton in the most salient ways.

The diningroom whispers with sophisticated laughter, a nod at certain waiters as they retreat to the kitchen, a hand of deeply red wine raised to toast the harpist. Everything white and mahogany and rightly presented, especially the food which is unrelentingly exquisite, no matter what it is. This particular night it was possibilities remoulade.

But the best part is the feeling that you're in the right place at the right time, whether such a situation makes you comfortable or not. With a minimum of luck, you see someone inferior upon whom you can cast silent aspersions. I never feel better than when I'm at Boomers. I love Boomer's beard and his blueberry vinaigrette. In his chef's hat and tie-less tux shirt, he breezes across the room with such an air of importance that you'd think every good idea ever invented, from gravity and pesto to existentialism, was his. You just know he'd claim every one of them if he thought he could get away with it.

Everyone knows the food at Boomers is incomparable. I sometimes hear complaints from those who think the servings are small, but when the cuisine is of the quality you'll find at Boomers, a little goes a long way. Others complain about the prices, but you get what you pay for, as the saying goes, and in this case what you pay for is the innovative wisdom and skill of a nationally recognized chef, a man so at home with food that he lives upstairs from the place he calls his "studio." A brilliant *cuisinier* demands his day at the bank.

Actually, Boomer doesn't want any more business than he already has, which makes him a hero of mine. That's why the service is, as Boomer says, slow and slovenly, downright insulting if that's what the customer requires. If it takes an hour to get your drink, perhaps you were meant to drink elsewhere that particular night.

But what service when someone does take your order! Where else will your server want to know your reaction to last night's edition of *The News Hour*, or complexity theory, or the new California kiwi industry.

Location (in the heart of the city's Bohemian district), decor (eclectic, to say the least), adventurous cuisine (swordfish cooked in Kaluha with creme fraiche, for example), stunning conversation (who, other than Fellini, would replace Boutros Boutros-Ghali as secretary general of the United Nations, and Fellini's already dead), and, of course, Boomer's own brand of jokery, as when he came to work in drag and stripped down to his work clothes. Then stripped further and cooked in his wife's bikini?

Come see. Come be seen. If you can't pull it off here, you obviously weren't meant to wear it.

Skippy's Family Restaurant
600 Towne Square
699-2100

Last Monday, Kitty and I ate at Skippy's. Wouldn't you know it would be "All you can eat night." (I seem to have a way of stumbling upon these events, especially when they're advertised.) I'll be the first to admit that Skipper doesn't always like to see me show up, knowing as he does how Kitty and I love to eat. He even tried to lock me out one night and said he wasn't kidding. And here I was all alone, just a puny one-half of Kitty's and my eating team.

Anyway, I can't speak highly enough of Skippy's, whether it's all you can eat night or not. The silverware's always clean, the napkins are perfectly folded, and the music is always turned down low enough that all you know is that it's of the elevator persuasion. The staff is always friendly and pretends to know you when they tell you it's been a long time since they saw you and ask how your children are, especially the one who was having trouble with spelling and the other one who was on the track team. It's all an act but it does add to the pleasant atmosphere at Skippy's.

The food, of course, speaks for itself.

There was boiled okra and tomatoes, fried okra, fried green tomatoes, and boiled okra all by itself with a few slices of seasoning bacon. Over on the salad bar, we saw *pickled* okra. There was no lack of okra.

Skipper had crowder peas, black-eyed peas, baby limas, butter beans, green pole beans cooked in meat grease, butter peas, buttered cabbage. There were four kinds of cornbread: skillet cake, sticks, fritters, and Mexican. He doesn't count his hush-puppies as a form of cornbread; "they was just hushpuppies all by their selves," as he puts it.

There was fried corn, rice, gravy, mashed potatoes, potato salad, new potatoes, baked potatoes, french fries, sweet potatoes, and squash casserole. Skipper had turnip greens, mustard greens, and collards.

Skipper himself is especially fond of his broccoli casserole. He boils his carrots in orange juice, which is different to most folks. Those are the only two things Skipper himself cooks. Everything else, he has the help do it.

There was fried catfish, fried pork chops, country fried steak, crispy fried chicken, regular fried chicken, chicken fingers, and chicken-vegetable soup. There was also chicken and dumplings and chicken pot pie, which Skipper likes to call Chicken Pot Cobbler, since it's mostly crust.

In addition to the four kinds of cornbread, Skipper has frozen rolls heated in the microwave, his mother-in-law's biscuits, hamburger rolls, and your normal sliced white bread. And bread pudding as his lead-off dessert.

There's also rice pudding, banana pudding, and strawberry jello with pineapple chunks on top. There's lemon icebox pie, chocolate pie, and coconut pie. If Skipper has any dough left over from the blackberry or peach cobbler, he makes apple fried pies.

The next time Skipper tries to lock me out, I'll just stand there and pound on the door as long as I have to. As I said, the food speaks for itself. Kitty speaks for it, too. And it's only eight bucks, more or less.

About the author

Fred Bonnie grew up in Maine and lived in Alabama for twenty-two years. A former garden editor for Southern Living and an advertising executive for a Birmingham software company, the author has also worked as a dishwasher, short-order cook, bartender, chef, pizza deliveryman, and caterer. Mr. Bonnie presently lives in North Carolina.